MISSIONARY MOMENTS

MISSIONARY MOMENTS

KEVIN STOKER

Bookcraft
Salt Lake City, Utah

Library of Congress Catalog Card Number: 89-85672

ISBN 0-88494-702-5

First Printing, 1989

Printed in the United States of America

Contents

III: TEACHING BY EXAMPLE

IV: MEMBER MISSIONARIES

V: BOOK OF MORMON CONVERSIONS

VI: "COINCIDENCES" OF CONVERSION

VII: THE SPIRIT CONVERTS

VIII: LONG-TIME CONVERSIONS

I

Missionaries

1

A Boy's Blessing Fulfilled

With the stake patriarch's hands on his head, the young boy from Whitney, Idaho, received an answer to his prayer that he might serve the Lord. "He promised me if I were worthy, I would be called on a mission to foreign countries," recalled President Ezra Taft Benson, who would become the thirteenth President of the Church on November 10, 1985, at age eighty-six. In his blessing "the patriarch said I would go to the nations of the world and preach the gospel and many people would rise up and bless my name because of the influence I would have in bringing them into the Church."

After more than four decades as an Apostle, President Benson can look back and see the fulfillment of his blessing. In that time, he reestablished the European Mission following World War II and traveled across the globe on other Church assignments.

But in 1921, when he accepted a mission call to Great Britain, he probably couldn't conceive of the import of his blessing. He was twenty-one when he arrived in Great Britain that August 1, and was assigned to the Newcastle Conference in northern England, near the Scottish border.

For the next two years he labored in the Newcastle area, serving as conference president for the last ten months of his mission. He served under two mission presidents: Orson F. Whitney and David O. McKay, both members of the Council of the Twelve.

According to mission records, he had been in the field two months when he and Elder Ralph S. Gray baptized three people.

The missionaries endured strong anti-Mormon sentiment spread by the news media and expressed by the general populace of the time. President Benson said that dealing with hostile crowds as a missionary better equipped him to handle the challenges of public office. As President Dwight D. Eisenhower's secretary of agriculture for eight years, he often came under fire for his policies, and his speeches were sometimes interrupted by hecklers. His ability to stay calm and courteous in these situations impressed even the media.

"I was possibly better prepared for abuse than the average man because of my faith in prayer and my religious training," he told a reporter in 1958. "An important part of my work [as a missionary] was preaching in the mining and factory district, and I can testify that a British mineworker fresh from the pub can out-heckle anyone else in the world."

2

Rock-Throwing Lessons

Late in 1955, Elder Roger Beitler and his companion met stiff opposition as they tried to open the Brazilian city of Piracicaba to missionary work. Every day for a month, a local religious leader used his afternoon radio program to preach against the Mormons. But this anti-Mormon fervor would soon provide an opportunity for Elder Beitler, serving in only his first area, to hurl the work forward in a remarkable way.

The missionaries had spent most of their time proselyting with little success in the center of Piracicaba. Hoping that people in another area might be more receptive, they boarded a bus bound for the south end of the city. The bus line ended in a *praca* (square) next to a large Catholic church. The missionaries stepped off the bus at about the same time several padres came out of the church. The padres, who had just finished their monthly meeting, stopped and stared at the two Americans. "In those days," Elder Beitler recalls, "the missionaries were required to wear hats, and I had a beautiful white Panama. I doffed my hat and said, 'Good morning, fathers.' They all twirled around and rushed back into the church."

The elders continued down a hill and began knocking on doors in a new residential area. As the missionaries went from door to door, they were followed by an increasing number of children. A lady, calling herself a believer (Protestant), invited the elders in for a drink of water. She was kind, but not too interested in their message. They were about to leave, when a loud commotion outside caused the lady to look out the window. She gasped and advised them to stay. Waiting to confront the missionaries was an unruly mob that now included more adults than children. At the head of the crowd was a padre wearing a long, black robe.

"We decided we couldn't hide there all day, so we walked out the door and were met with shouts of derision," Elder Beitler remembers. His companion warned him to stay at his side and then walked toward the padre. The padre and the mob retreated before the missionaries. The companion smiled, then took off his hat and said, "Good morning, father. May I help you?" When the padre could back up no further, he replied, "Yes, you can help me. You can help me by leaving this area and never coming back." The elders continued to smile as they slowly turned around and headed up the hill toward the bus stop. Moments later, Elder Beitler heard the sound of something whizzing through the air and clattering against the street.

"We're being stoned," he thought. "I can't believe it. They stoned Stephen! They stoned Paul! And now I, Roger Beitler, am being stoned."

His euphoria and exhilaration ended abruptly when a rock struck him hard in the shoulder. Whipping his six-foot-two, two-hundred-pound frame around, he picked up a rock, and reared back to throw it at the padre leading the group. "Not a person moved. Not a sound was made. I had that rock in my hand, and I weighed it, up and down, flexing my fingers around it, all the time looking that padre straight in the eye." The young missionary, a former semipro baseball pitcher, had no doubt he could strike his target. "But," he thought, "I haven't come all the way to Brazil to throw rocks at people. I'm here to teach the gospel."

About one hundred feet away, he spied a metal utility pole and fired the rock into the pole. "Waannng!" The metal shuddered at the impact.

"No music was ever sweeter to my ears," he recalls. "The people ceased to be a mob and now became spectators." One of the boys in the crowd threw a rock at the pole, missing it by a long distance. Then, others in the crowd began hurling rocks wildly at the pole, but not one struck the metal. The elders also began throwing rocks at the pole, hitting it several times before picking up their hats and leaving without incident.

The next day, when the missionaries returned to the area, they were met by several boys who asked if they would teach them how to throw rocks. After that, a pile of rocks was waiting for the missionaries whenever they were in the area. "Pretty soon, when we came to the doors of people in the area, the parents would say, 'You must be the Americans who know how to throw rocks; I've been curious about you, come in.' And for the first time, missionary work progressed in that town."

Twenty years later, in 1975, President Roger Beitler of the Brazil São Paulo South Mission interviewed a missionary, who happened to be from the Piracicaba Ward. President Beitler asked where the meetinghouse was located. "You know where the *praca* is on the south side of town, across the river?" the elder said. "You go down the hill from the Catholic church, and where [the area] flattens out . . . , we now have one of the most beautiful chapels in all of Brazil."

3

Always a Missionary

He was the Presiding Bishop of the Church in 1949, but in his heart and speech LeGrand Richards was still a full-time missionary, a foot soldier of the Lord, boldly preaching the message of the restored gospel.

"I have had so many experiences," he said at a general priesthood meeting that year, "that I cannot understand why we cannot plant the truth in the hearts of our people until no outside thing or movement in the world can have any influence with them. We have so much more to offer than any other church in the world."

During that address, he told about holding a street meeting in an Eastern city in 1926, where another church was holding a convention a short distance away. Some of that church's ministers tried to break up the LDS meeting. Elder Richards defused the situation by offering the ministers thirty minutes to speak at the end of the meeting.

During their thirty minutes, the ministers said the Mormons "would bind the Book of Mormon in the same cover with the Bible and ask us to take it and like it." When they finished, Elder Richards told the crowd of two hundred to three hundred people that the following Tuesday he would tell why the Mormons would bind the Book of Mormon with the Bible.

A week later, the crowd was larger than before. Elder Richards, using the Bible, quoted Ezekiel about combining the sticks of Judah and Joseph. He testified that the Book of Mormon was the record of Joseph's descendants. "As I remember, we sold sixteen copies of the Book of Mormon that night," he said.

On another occasion in that same city Elder Richards taught a lady he had met with several times before. "Mr. Richards," she said, "are you trying to make Mormons out of all of us?" Elder Richards said he would never ask her to join the Church. But, he added, "If I could show you where you could trade a dollar for five dollars, I would not have to ask you to do it, would I?" After returning home from his mission, he received a letter from the lady in which she wrote, "I decided to trade the dollar for five dollars. I was baptized last Friday."

Elder Richards, who served as an Apostle for thirty-one years before his death in 1983, said, "I think that any elder in Israel who cannot make Mormonism look better than five to one had better get hold of the scriptures and go to work and study the gospel."

4

A Prophecy Fulfilled

Claudius V. Spencer had a feeling he was going to be called on a mission, so he stayed away from the April 1850 conference until the last session. He figured that if he wasn't seen he might be forgotten. He went to the door, opened it a few inches, and peered inside just in time to see one of the Brethren arise on the stand and say: "It is moved and seconded that Claudius V. Spencer go on a mission to Europe."

"I turned as though shot," Claudius said. "[I] walked down Main Street saying to myself, 'Can it be possible those men have any inspiration to call such a stick for a missionary?' "

Most of the missionaries called in those days were large and powerful physical specimens. But Claudius was small and skinny. How could they call him? he thought. Nobody had ever heard him pray or speak in public. But as with David, the Lord didn't measure Claudius by his physical stature but by his heart. And through a blessing given by President Heber C. Kimball, a counselor in the First Presidency, a promise was given to the reluctant missionary that he would preach like the Apostle Paul and then return to Zion bringing many "sheaves" with him.

Elder Spencer became a powerful missionary and a forceful orator. On one occasion, the president of the Norwich Branch hesitated to bring the diminutive missionary into his home because his wife and nine children had yet to accept the gospel. He feared Elder Spencer would be hurt. Upon hearing this, the missionary turned to the branch leader and asked for an invitation. "If you do so, I promise you in the name of the Lord that every one of your family shall embrace the gospel, and every one shall live to go to Zion; if you do not, and have not faith to stand up in your place as the head of your own family, you are not fit to stand as president of the branch; and more than that, you will apostatize and none of you be saved in the kingdom of God." The branch leader invited Elder Spencer to his home, and soon his family joined the Church and emigrated to Zion.

At another time during his mission, Elder Spencer felt prompted to open a nearby town to the gospel. Before he left for the town, he counseled with the local branch president and elders in the city where Elder Spencer was serving. "If you go to that place," the branch president warned, "I clear myself of the consequences; your blood be upon your own head." Elder Spencer asked for volunteers to go with him. Finally, the youngest elder in the conference (district) promised to meet him there. The town was about thirty-seven miles away from conference headquarters. Elder Spencer walked the distance in a little more than a day, arriving late in the morning. After gaining permission to speak in the only suitable building, Elder Spencer went from door to door, notifying the people of the meeting. The young elder arrived as promised, but soon left because a crowd of children followed them through the streets, jeering and throwing dry manure and pieces of coal at them.

That evening the building was crowded with people and many others were congregated outside. When the missionary arrived, he was struck in the head by a large piece of peat sod and knocked down. He said a prayer, arose, and pressed his way into the building, declaring he was there to deliver a lecture. He spoke with a touching eloquence, bringing tears to the eyes of many in attendance. At the end of the meeting, a minister tried to berate the Mormon elder, but the congregation "hoisted the [minister] out of the building and hooted him home." Four weeks later, Elder Spencer organized a branch in the town with sixteen members.

Later, while presiding over the Norwich Conference, Elder Spencer learned about a huge anti-Mormon meeting at St. Andrew's Hall. Ignoring protests from friends, he went to the meeting. The room was densely packed with more than two thousand people. Seventeen prominent ministers from Norfolk and Suffolk sat on the stand. The missionary boldly walked to the stand and sat down behind the ministers. More than three hours passed before the chairman asked if any Mormons in the audience had the "hardihood and moral courage" to defend their faith.

"Of course, all eyes had been on me, and the invitation was a trap on the part of the ministers," Elder Spencer recorded later. "They offered me no way of getting to the pulpit as I was behind five rows of seats, each of which was packed with my opponents and not one offered to allow me to pass. I prayed, put my hands on the sides of the heads of the two ministers in front of me, made an opening, and stepped over into their seat. This I did with the others until I reached the pulpit."

Elder Spencer didn't remember much of the things he said, but as he finished his oration, he was facing the ministers and declaring: "You are infidels, and it is you who make infidels, and by your precepts smother the hope of any realization of the gifts and blessings promised by Christ and His Apostles. I prophesy, moreover, to you in the name of the Lord Jesus Christ, that your labors of this day and night, shall be the cause of hundreds embracing the gospel I preach." When Elder Spencer sat down, the chairman of the meeting tried to read from the Book of Mormon, but he shook so badly that he couldn't read. Another attempted to speak but barely uttered a word.

After the meeting, a mob formed, "acting more like devils than men." Members of the mob looked for Elder Spencer but seemed blinded to his presence. However, a tall man wearing a long cloak did see him and covered the slight missionary with his cloak and helped him escape.

As Elder Spencer had prophesied, the work prospered. At the end of his three-year mission in early 1853, the Norwich Conference had 1,059 members. Of those, 150 people had been baptized in the last six months. When Elder Spencer returned to Utah, he brought with him ninety-five souls, thus fulfilling the final part of President Heber C. Kimball's promise.

5

A History of the Indians

When President George Albert Smith was twenty-one, he served as a missionary in South Carolina. At that time he gave a Book of Mormon to a man who became instrumental in helping missionaries for the next fifteen years.

Elder Smith had just visited some seriously ill elders in Columbia, South Carolina. He was returning by train when he met the man. As the train was passing an Indian settlement, Elder Smith tapped the shoulder of the man sitting in front of him and asked, "Do you know what Indians these are?"

The man replied, "They are the Catawbas."

"Do you know where they came from?"

The middle-aged man replied that nobody knew where Indians came from. Elder Smith then interjected, "They came from Jerusalem six hundred years before the birth of Christ."

"Where did you get that information?" the man asked.

"From the history of the Indians," Elder Smith said. The man thought the young man was putting one over on him.

"Where is this history?"

Elder Smith pulled out a Book of Mormon and handed it to the man. After browsing through it, the man offered to buy the book, but the future Church president resisted.

"I will be on the train for three hours," he said. "You can read it for that long, and it won't cost you anything."

After reading some of the book, the man turned and said, "I don't want to give up this book."

Elder Smith said he couldn't sell it because it was his last copy, but the man could take the book if he would send it back after three weeks.

Two weeks later, Elder Smith received a letter from the man saying he still wanted to buy the book. The elder wrote back and told him to keep it with his compliments.

Fifteen years later, Elder Smith and Elder B. H. Roberts were visiting the Southern States Mission when they were sought out by an Associated Press official who offered his services to the elders. The official turned out to be the man Elder Smith had befriended on the train.

Since reading the Book of Mormon, the man had become a friend of the Church, working to keep missionaries out of jail and free from mobs.

6

A Lifelong Missionary

Gerald W. Smith is a Scotland Yard detective from London, England, and Bessie M. De Long is a homemaker from Grain Valley, Missouri. They have never met. But when the *Church News* printed a story on January 16, 1988, about Brother Smith's conversion to the Church and his work in law enforcement, it struck Sister De Long so strongly, that she said, "I just had to sit down and write [to the *Church News*]."

She recalled how in March 1956 she was a less-active member of the Independence Branch in Independence, Missouri, who "didn't want to be found." Her husband was a member of another faith, and their two sons attended services with him.

During a trip to Seattle, Washington, that year, they stayed overnight in Salt Lake City, Utah.

"I asked my husband the next morning if we could take a tour of Temple Square," she recalled, "and to my surprise, he said yes. After we finished the tour, we ended up in the museum with a young tour guide standing with his back to the big window, and with the temple behind him, bearing his testimony and holding the standard works.

"I have thought of this young returned missionary many times over the years," she wrote. "I talked with him privately that day as my husband and sons were wandering around the museum. He gave me a book, *The Articles of Faith* by James E. Talmage, and he put his name and address in it."

Following their visit to Temple Square, the De Longs seemed to have "one miracle after another" occur in their lives. In March 1957, Bessie De Long's husband and sons were baptized into the Church.

What makes these two seemingly unrelated conversion stories similar is the fact that it was the same Temple Square tour guide, Calvin C. Cook, who introduced the detective from England and the family from Missouri to the gospel. From 1947 until his death in 1982, Brother Cook shared his testimony with thousands of people as a tour guide on Temple Square.

"He probably was released two or three times, but he managed to wangle his way back on the staff," said his wife, Nadine Cook. "He was a missionary through and through. My husband was kind of notorious for asking our daughters' dates if they were going on missions."

No doubt many people throughout the world love Calvin Cook for the testimony he gave that helped change their lives and bring them into the Church.

7

The Golden Contact

Near the end of January 1985, Sister Dzidra Yallouris, a fifty-nine-year-old single missionary serving in the Arkansas Little Rock Mission, fervently prayed to be led to a "golden contact." It wasn't the first time on her mission she had asked to be led to someone prepared to hear the gospel. Having taught and seen baptized a golden contact in Jackson, Tennessee, in the fall of 1984, she knew exactly the type of person she wanted to find.

In a few days her prayer was answered. While proselyting where the Spirit prompted them to go, she and her companion, Sister Marilyn E. Cooper, were led to a home in Jonesboro, Arkansas. "We knocked on the door, and a smiling, gracious woman opened it and said, 'Come in,' " Sister Yallouris recalls. "It seemed as if she had expected us."

The missionaries taught the first discussion and made an appointment to return. As they were leaving, the investigator said, "I want to be baptized."

"This lady, Rosemary Andrews, had been prepared by the Lord for the gospel," Sister Yallouris says. "Within a week we gave her all the discussions. She received them with an open heart and mind, and she believed it. The Spirit was strong while we were teaching her."

The baptismal date was set for February 9, 1985. On February 7 the sisters visited Rosemary and discovered that some evangelists had called her and warned her not to join the Mormon church. They said that they were coming to see her and tell her all about the Mormon religion and its doctrine. "We had hardly sat down, and here they came," Sister Yallouris remembers.

First to walk in was a large woman about three times the size of Sister Yallouris. She packed a worn Bible under her arm. The evangelist was followed by her husband and another woman. "Now I know how David must have felt when he was facing Goliath in battle," the missionary thought. "My companion and I looked at each other, and our hearts sank to our heels. I began to pray silently, pleading to the Lord for help. 'Oh, Heavenly Father, what must we do? How will we face this lady and her companions? They most likely know the Bible very well and will try to talk Rosemary out of joining the Church. Oh, please help us, Heavenly Father.' "

As she prayed, Sister Yallouris felt her fear replaced by a sweet, calm feeling. Her companion opened the discussion with prayer and had barely said "Amen" when the evangelist began telling Rosemary why she shouldn't join the Church.

"Suddenly," Sister Yallouris says, "the large lady stopped talking. She shut her eyes and tried to open her mouth, but no sound came out. She was grasping for words. A Christlike love filled my heart, and I began to talk. I told them about my conversion. I told them about the gospel and the restored Church. The man even asked a few questions. I finished by bearing my testimony."

All the while Sister Yallouris talked, the evangelist frantically tore through the pages of her Bible, trying to find a scripture. The sisters taught for more than two hours, and the large woman's frustration grew as she continued to rustle through her scriptures. Finally, Sister Yallouris asked her what scripture she wanted to find. She said Galatians 1:6–12. The missionary helped the evangelist find the passage, which happened to be the same one the missionaries had read to Rosemary the day before.

Sister Yallouris asked the evangelist to give a closing prayer, and she accepted. After she finished praying, she scooped up her Bible and quietly departed. From the beginning, Rosemary had watched and listened to the spectacle in silence. Now she and the missionaries marveled at the way the Lord had answered their prayers. Two days later Rosemary was baptized and confirmed a member of The Church of Jesus Christ of Latter-day Saints.

8

Blessed for Obedience

Eben R. T. Blomquist and his brother wanted to go to the circus, but they had already agreed to go with their mother to a Mormon meeting in Malmö, Sweden. At the meeting, two missionaries told of the restoration of the Church through Joseph Smith. "A new world opened up," Eben Blomquist later wrote. "It was all so interesting that my brother and I agreed it was much better than if we had gone to the circus."

The family started attending meetings regularly. On one occasion, the discussion was on the Word of Wisdom. Eben Blomquist was so impressed that he vowed on that day, January 19, 1905, never to drink coffee, tea, or liquor, and never to use tobacco.

On July 8, 1906, the Blomquist family was baptized in the ocean. Two years later they immigrated to Utah.

In 1911, Eben returned to Sweden as a missionary. He arrived to find that the government, under pressure from the state religion, had deported the mission president.

One by one the missionaries were called to the police station to be interviewed. The first question asked was, "Are you an American citizen?" If the police discovered Elder Blomquist was a Swedish citizen, he would be conscripted into the army. "I prayed that I would not be asked that question," Eben said. "When my turn came I was asked only my name."

Later in his mission, Elder Blomquist and his companion were arrested and jailed in the town of Växjö for preaching Mormon doctrine. The town's church council ruled that the elders would be fined three hundred kronor (about three hundred dollars) if they kept preaching.

Gaining permission to speak, Elder Blomquist quoted Acts 5:28–29, 32: "Did not we straitly command you that ye should not teach in his name? . . . Then Peter and the other apostles answered and said, We ought to obey God rather than men. . . . And we are his witnesses of these things; and so is also the Holy Ghost. . . ."

Despite more arrests, Elder Blomquist was able to complete his mission. Later in his life, he served six more missions—three as a mission president.

9

Free to Preach the Gospel

Nearly eight years after the Church sent missionaries to Recife, Brazil, it had only established two branches in this city of two million on Brazil's northeastern coast. In January 1974, six full-time missionaries were serving in the metropolitan area, two of them native Brazilians. One of the elders, Howard Fish, recalls how each Wednesday afternoon at rush hour, the missionaries would go to the large, busy Praca (town square) da Independencia in downtown Recife and conduct a street meeting.

"We each would take a turn standing up and, in a loud voice, preach a gospel message (usually a segment from the missionary discussions) to any and all passersby. The other five would 'hit up' the people as they passed our little meeting."

Many of the people showed interest in the missionaries' message, but others just wanted to argue with the elders or ridicule their beliefs. On January 16, 1974, one of these street meetings provided Elder Fish with the most frightening, yet exhilarating experience of his mission.

Elder Joao Roberto Grahl, a zone leader from Novo Hamburgo, Brazil, had drawn a large crowd in the middle of the square. Elder Grahl's powerful sermons always seemed to attract more listeners than all the other missionaries combined. Elder Donald Fry of Bremerton, Washington, had just replaced the Brazilian elder when a commotion erupted in the center of the crowd. A man in a gray suit, identifying himself as a police detective, had accosted two of the missionaries and ordered them to stop preaching in public. "He also wanted all six of us to go with him to the police station, where he was going to sign a complaint against us," Elder Fish remembers. "Suddenly, two things occurred to me: that there was a very large crowd gathered around us of about one hundred people, and that we six elders could very possibly be on our way to jail. The latter thought frightened me considerably."

The two Brazilian missionaries, Elders Grahl and Orlando Albuquerque, of São Paulo, were not intimidated by the threat. Instead, they marched the man in the gray suit over to two military policemen who were standing guard in the *praca*. Most of the crowd followed them. Elder Albuquerque told the policemen that the laws of Brazil permitted the missionaries to assemble and preach in the square.

"To our great astonishment," Elder Fish says, "many in the crowd began to yell, 'Let them preach!' 'Their message is about God!' 'Brazil is a free nation!' "

The two policemen conferred. They then told the missionaries they could continue preaching. "A loud roar went up from the crowd as many yelled to us, 'Yes, yes, let's go preach,' " Elder Fish marvels. "We were nearly carried back to our original place on the *praca* by the large throng."

The missionaries later discovered that the man in the gray suit was not a police detective at all. He was a government motion-picture censor who had been prodded by two ministers to halt the elders. But such efforts to stop the Lord's work in Recife only caused it to move forward more rapidly. Several stakes have since been organized and a mission established in the city.

Elder Fish feels the incident at the *praca* was a partial fulfillment of Elder Melvin J. Ballard's dedication on Christmas Day 1925 of the South American continent to the preaching of the gospel. "Bless . . . the leading officials of these South American countries, that they may kindly receive us and give us permission to open the doors of salvation to the people of these lands. . . . And do rebuke and command to be stayed every power that would oppose the preaching of the gospel in these lands."

10

A Generous Employer

As they walked along a New England country road in the mid-1940s, Elders Truman Madsen and Reuel J. Bawden wondered where they would get their next meal.

The missionaries "were rather unpopular among these farm folk," writes Elder Madsen of the experience. The two missionaries had spent the night sleeping in a barn and hadn't eaten in twenty-four hours. So they left the road and entered a grove of trees to pray for help in getting something to eat.

"This happened often in our country work—going off into the woods to pray," writes Elder Madsen. "It wasn't a habit—it was a necessity. Who but the Lord could help us in these hostile country areas? We were without purse or scrip. But He in whose work we were engaged was ever within reach, the unfailing source."

In the prayer, Elder Bawden pleaded, "Father, wilt thou open the way for us to have a bite to eat."

As they arose, the elders saw a trout jump and strike a fly in the small brook flowing through the grove of trees.

"O for a fishing pole!" Elder Madsen muttered.

"What's wrong with what you have in your hands?" queried Elder Bawden.

The tattered umbrella didn't look like much, but it was all they had. Elder Bawden doubled up some thread and attached a doctored safety pin to the end while his companion located a worm. Elder Madsen then gave the contraption a try.

Dangling the line over the grassy bank, he thought, "Can this be the way the Lord is going to answer our prayer . . . , or do I just have a flair for the unusual?"

He already knew the answer. The Lord had answered their prayers before, so there was no reason why he couldn't arrange for a fish to bite.

Wham! A trout struck hard. Elder Madsen jerked, and a fish flew over his head, off the hook and onto the bank. As they looked for more worms, tears filled their eyes.

They caught and cooked six fish, offering heartfelt thanks to the Lord before eating them, fins and all.

"You know," said Elder Bawden as he picked up his suitcase, "the Lord is a mighty generous employer."

11

Clothes Didn't Matter

In the early 1900s, the missionary force of the Church consisted of men like Erastus Christian Willardson, who was called to serve in Denmark two weeks after his fourth child had died at birth.

In the homeland of his parents, Elder Willardson and his companion labored among family members still living in the country. During visits to his companion's relatives, the two separated for a brief time. The companion wanted to teach his rich uncle but feared that Elder Willardson's worn clothes, though neat and clean, would make a bad impression on the uncle. While Elder Willardson stayed at the home of his companion's aunt, his fellow missionary traveled to see the influential Dane.

"This didn't seem just right to me, because the elders are counseled to go out two by two," Elder Willardson said. "I kneeled down in a bunch of willows and told my Heavenly Father about the circumstance, and prayed that my companion and I could be together again."

The companion soon returned to his aunt's house, having found that his uncle wasn't home. When the missionary arrived, the wealthy uncle, who had come to visit his sister, was there. The uncle was captivated by the elders' message and invited them to his home. He also provided for their transportation to Aarhus, their next assignment.

Later, in a letter, the uncle said Elder Willardson was the most impressive missionary he had ever met.

In Aarhus, Elder Willardson was arrested and given a choice: thirty days in prison, or banishment. He chose the latter but received permission to visit relatives before leaving the country. He risked going back to Aarhus to baptize an investigator named Alfred Miller.

After almost drowning while performing the baptism in an icy river, Elder Willardson confirmed Alfred and then rushed to catch a train. As he and Alfred were walking down the street, they saw standing under a street light the policeman who had arrested the elders.

When they passed, the policeman didn't see Elder Willardson. But then, neither did Alfred.

"As we passed [the policeman]," Alfred said, "I looked to where you were, but I was unable to see you, though you were six feet tall and of heavy build."

12

'Your God Is a God of Power'

On the night of May 5, 1852, Elder James S. Brown and his handful of Polynesian converts held a testimony meeting, then prayed. They didn't sleep, because outside the Mormons' meeting place, a mob of young braves were boasting of roasting the "fat missionary" while they danced and yelled through the night. Elder Brown had encountered fierce opposition since coming to Raivavae, a small island located more than four hundred miles south of Tahiti. Now the island leaders had decided during the night to burn the Mormon missionary.

On the afternoon of May 6, two large warriors armed with clubs burst into the hut and took Elder Brown to the beach. Most of the island's people had gathered there, with about thirty old councilors and fifteen stout warriors standing near a large, burning pile of wood and coral. In front of the boisterous crowd of islanders stood the missionary and his faithful converts. Stepping toward the mob, a convert named Rivae declared: "If you burn this man, you burn me first." His wife, holding her eight-month-old baby, rushed to his side and shouted, "I am a Mormon, and this baby is a Mormon, for 'nits make lice,' [a phrase used by the men who shot Mormon children at the Haun's Mill Massacre] and you will have to burn all of us, or Mormonism will grow again."

The leader of the opposition raced past the couple and confronted Elder Brown. Motioning to the now blistering bonfire, the chief bellowed: "Look, there is the fire. It is made to consume the flesh off your bones."

At that moment, Elder Brown, under the influence of the Spirit, proclaimed: "In the name of Israel's God, I defy ten of your best men, yea, the host of you, for I serve that God who delivered

Daniel from the den of lions, and the three Hebrew children from the fiery furnace." As soon as he finished speaking, Elder Brown stood his ground before his accusers. The old councilors started verbally disputing with the young braves. Soon a fight broke out among them, and in the confusion that followed the Mormons slipped safely away.

Two months later, one of the old councilors ran away when he saw Elder Brown. The missionary chased the man down and asked him why he had fled. "Your God is a God of power, and I was afraid to meet His servant," the old native cried. Then he recalled the day the warriors had tried to burn the missionary. "At the moment that you defied us there was a brilliant light, or pillar of fire, [bearing] down close over your head. . . . We thought that you had prayed to your God of Power, and that he had sent the fire to burn us and our people if we harmed you. The young men did not see the light. They were going to burn you, and we tried to stop them. So we got into a fight."

13

The Fruits of Perseverance

On June 4, 1985, Elders Francisco Frausto and Luis Catron of the Spain Madrid Mission were enjoying their weekly preparation day when Elder Catron remembered they had an appointment that day at 11:00 A.M. "I wasn't very excited about having the appointment on 'P-day,' " recalled Francisco Frausto, after his mission, while living in the La Cienega Ward in California, "but I knew we should keep it."

The appointment was with Miguel Gento Rodriguez, a police officer, who had invited the missionaries to come to his home. But when the missionaries arrived, Rodriguez met them on the street near his home. He said he couldn't meet that day and asked them to come back the following day, June 5. "We felt discouraged, and didn't know whether he was sincere, but we went back anyway," Francisco says.

The next day, Miguel was home. He listened to the first discussion and stopped smoking and drinking that night. After two more discussions in two days, he told the elders that he was leaving on a one-month vacation. "Again we wondered—was he being straightforward, or was he trying to get rid of us?"

The missionaries fasted and prayed many times while Miguel was away, hoping he would retain his interest in the gospel. On the day he returned from his vacation, Miguel visited with the missionaries. "He told us that he had taken the Book of Mormon with him, and had read from the beginning through the Words of Mormon," relates Francisco.

On the next visit, Miguel asked the missionaries to teach his wife, Estrella. She gradually gained interest but struggled to quit smoking. The missionaries fasted and prayed in her behalf, and she was able to stop. On August 11, 1985, Miguel was baptized. A week later, he received the priesthood, and a week after that he baptized his wife. He later became president of the Palencia Branch in Spain, and Sister Rodriguez later served as Relief Society president.

Participating in these conversions taught Francisco that any sacrifices the missionaries may have made were "superficial when compared to the great joy we experienced with Miguel and Estrella."

"Teaching them," says Francisco, "helped me gain a testimony that perseverance does bring blessings."

14

Rescued by Strangers

Elders David and Amasa Howard were going home.

From 1910–13, they had preached the restored gospel to the people of England. Now David was bound for the town of Nuneaton to meet his brother and enjoy a farewell party with local members and missionaries before sailing for America.

But their joyful reunion was short-lived, and their celebration never materialized. Instead, the brothers met just in time to discover the Church meetinghouse surrounded by nearly five hundred angry people itching for a fight.

The people were upset because a local family—a mother, her four daughters, and a son—had recently left town with a "Mormon elder" headed for Utah. Many in the mob were saying the missionary had taken the women back to Utah for immoral purposes.

Amasa had the misfortune of looking like the missionary who had helped the family immigrate, and David had the misfortune of being Amasa's brother. When the mob saw the brothers, they seized them and dragged them toward the river. Leaders of the crowd declared that they would drown the Mormons. The rioters beat Amasa and David with sticks and clubs every step of the way. Amasa was stabbed in the back with a knife but was not seriously injured.

Several policemen came to the brothers' rescue, but the mob was so large and unruly that even the lawmen backed off, leaving the pair to face the people's wrath alone.

The mob, kicking and shoving its helpless quarry, was nearing the river when three young men, whom no one recognized, tore into the crowd with such strength and force that the people retreated and let them through. The stout strangers opened a pathway through the angry mob, allowing Amasa and David to dash through a door and enter an archway fronting the street. They then climbed over a back fence and escaped down an alley.

"I shall always believe that those three young men were not just ordinary men, but were sent from our Heavenly Father for our deliverance," wrote David several years later. "They were able to hold back a mob still consisting of some three hundred fifty enraged people. Such strength is not given man, but is given by our Heavenly Father for the deliverance of His servants."

15

No Better Place to Die

The Korean District of the Northern Far East Mission had been open only three years when President Paul C. Andrus went to Seoul, Korea, to decide whether to withdraw the missionaries from the country.

It was 1958. Beggars were everywhere. The scars of the Korean War were still apparent in bombed-out buildings and crowded, makeshift housing. The handful of LDS missionaries suffered from harsh living conditions and poor diets.

Of the ten missionaries who met with President Andrus, half had hepatitis. F. Ray Hawkins, one of Korea's first missionaries, said all three of the elders he traveled with to the meeting had this ailment. "One was told by the doctors that he couldn't expect to live, and if he wanted to die at home he should leave the country immediately," Ray Hawkins recalls.

President Andrus told the missionaries that he and their parents, along with the General Authorities, feared for the elders' health. He asked for the missionaries' feelings about closing the Korean District. Each elder responded that he felt the Lord had called him to Korea and that he should stay. "Those who were sick, in particular, stood and said they felt if it meant giving up their lives for the sake of the work, they couldn't think of a better place to die than in the mission field."

After all the elders had spoken, President Andrus arose, saying he felt the same way the missionaries did. He then read Doctrine and Covenants 103:27–28: "Let no man be afraid to lay down his life for my sake; for whoso layeth down his life for my sake shall find it again. And whoso is not willing to lay down his life for my sake is not my disciple."

Ray Hawkins, who later served as president of the Korea Seoul Mission, says he has never felt a greater outpouring of the Spirit than in that meeting. Most of the sick elders soon recovered, and then completed their missions.

Four years later, in 1962, the Korean Mission was created.

Korea now has a temple and tens of thousands of Church members in numerous stakes and missions.

16

A Little Child Shall Lead Them

Work among the Spanish-speaking majority of Argentina in 1925 seemed to be going nowhere. Elder Melvin J. Ballard of the Council of the Twelve and Elder Rey L. Pratt had searched Buenos Aires for two months before even finding a place to meet. Then, to their frustration, only children showed up to hear about the restored gospel.

It was the Church's second attempt to establish a mission in South America. The first, led by Elder Parley P. Pratt to Chile in 1851, failed after only six months. "He was not so fortunate as we were, because we had his grandson, Brother Rey L. Pratt, who is a master of the Spanish language," said Elder Ballard in the October 1926 general conference. "That enabled us to do a work that Brother Parley was unable to do."

However, the elders' initial success occurred among the German-speaking people of Argentina. A third member of the missionary party, Elder Rulon S. Wells, spoke German, and six German-speaking people were baptized before he became ill and returned to the United States.

Living among the German-speaking Saints on the outskirts of Buenos Aires, the elders traveled two hours by streetcar, then walked two miles on unpaved streets, on lanes, through fields, in mud, in dust, and in all kinds of weather to work with the Spanish-speaking people.

"And then when we did this, all we could get to come to our meetings, for nearly two months, were children," Elder Ballard said. Despite the difficulties, they resolved not to abandon their efforts to reach the people. Elder Ballard told how they then learned anew that "a little child shall lead them" (Isaiah 11:6).

"We continued with those children, teaching them to sing, teaching them to pray, to repeat the Lord's Prayer, the Articles of Faith, and the Ten Commandments," Elder Ballard said. The children carried these prayers and songs into their homes. Soon one parent showed up at the meeting hall, then another, and another, until the missionaries were able to organize a group meeting of adults.

Elder Ballard said the process was repeated in other areas and the work soon moved forward into the parents' homes.

II

On the Lord's Errand

17

Convinced Behind Bars

In September 1852, seven missionaries, some newly called, sailed the small sloop "Zion's Löve" from Denmark to Brevig on the coast of Norway. As they were nearing the city of Brevig, they were surprised to see Elder John A. Ahmanson and Priest Jeppe J. Folkmann coming toward them in a small skiff. With only a handful of Mormon missionaries serving in Norway at the time, this chance meeting two miles off the Norwegian coast was a remarkable and fortuitous coincidence.

Elder Ahmanson and Priest Folkmann had been confined in the Brevig prison for four days for preaching the gospel. They had just been liberated and were on their way to visit a family of investigators living across the water. "They were expecting us," recalled Elder Christian Larsen, "but did not know when we would arrive."

The two missionaries reported that Brevig was in an uproar, and a mob had threatened to kill the next "Mormon Priest" who might attempt to set foot on shore. Rumors had spread that more Mormon ministers were coming, and a group of seven landing at the same time could have been disastrous. The missionaries expressed thanks to the Lord for protecting His servants from their enemies. Deciding then to change course, they sailed to the nearby fishing village of Bauen. Some of the group debarked there and went further up shore to pray. When they returned they found their brethren engaged in prayer and singing hymns. After counseling together, the group decided Elder Johan F. F. Dorius would stay and preach in Brevig while the others sailed to Frederikstad.

These first Mormon missionaries enjoyed great success establishing the Church in Norway. But they also faced stiff opposition.

Norway had a state religion, but tolerated different denominations and doctrines if they qualified under law as "Christian dissenters." The Mormon missionaries fully expected to be classified as such, but the opposition, spearheaded by established clergy, cried out to the civil authorities that the Mormons were not Christians, and stridently called for their arrest and imprisonment.

Most of the missionaries refused to be intimidated. When Elder Christian Larsen reported at the police station in Österrisör to show his pass (visa), he was warned against preaching and threatened with imprisonment. He responded to the officers by testifying to the truthfulness of his message. He, Elder Ahmanson, and Elder Svend Larsen held ten meetings in the city, baptized seven people, administered to the sick, and strengthened the branch in Österrisör.

Later in Vaterland, a suburb of Frederikstad, Elder Christian Larsen and other members were hounded by hecklers during their meetings. They sought help from the city's mayor, but he said it was permissible to oppose "Mormon doctrines." Soon most of the missionaries were locked behind bars on charges that they had "administered the sacrament and preached."

After proselyting in Brevig, Johan Dorius journeyed to Frederikstad and began holding meetings. He was arrested and taken to prison. When he was walked into the jail cell, he discovered two of his brethren, Elders Christian and Svend Larsen, already there. In a few hours they were joined by Elder Peter Beckstrom. Despite their misfortune, the missionaries worried more about the work than their predicament.

"I rejoiced in being counted worthy to suffer for the gospel's sake, like my co-religionists in far-off America," Elder Christian Larsen recorded in his journal. "But I felt grieved in my spirit when I thought of the many noble souls who were anxious to learn of the things pertaining to the Kingdom of God, and that I was now deprived of the opportunity to instruct them."

His despair was eased by the companionship of his brethren. They passed the time by reading, singing, praying, conversing, and teaching the gospel to two men sharing their cell. The pair had also been arrested for preaching, and the missionaries took advantage of every opportunity to discuss the scriptures with them.

One, a Mr. Jacobsen, criticized and debated with the elders, but he was soon moved to another room.

The other man, Johan Andreas Jensen, tolerated the Mormons' views. At age five Jensen had gone to sea as a cabin boy. Over the next thirty years he had worked his way up to become captain of a large ship. In 1849 he gave most of his possessions to the poor and began to preach repentance to his countrymen. He had been thrown in jail for rebuking the king and the state religion.

At first the missionaries had no success teaching Johan. He seemed unimpressed with their doctrines until one Sunday morning when the jailer, a Mr. Fjeldstad, who had treated the missionaries with kindness, visited the cell with his son. Soon the men were embroiled in a lengthy conversation about religion.

"Elder Christian Larsen in particular testified to the truth of the gospel under the influence of the Holy Ghost and made a lasting impression on them [Jensen and Fjeldstad]," according to the *History of the Scandinavian Mission.* "After Mr. Fjeldstad left the cell, the brethren continued to converse with Mr. Jensen until they were all brought under a most pleasant and divine influence."

Johan burst into tears, declaring he knew what the missionaries were saying was true. His face seemed to shine with joy. On February 25, 1854, Johan was baptized. Nine years later he immigrated to America and pulled a handcart to Utah. He settled in Ephraim, where one of his daughters married Andrew C. Nelson. The Nelsons' grandson, Elder Russell M. Nelson, was sustained as a member of the Council of the Twelve on April 7, 1984.

18

Rocks Never Thrown

All Neils Peter Hjorth wanted to do was chase the missionaries out of town. Little did he realize that because of the message of these American elders, he would freely give up his home and country to immigrate to Zion.

In the mid-1800s, Neils, a blacksmith, lived with his family in Nørager, Denmark. The Hjorths were religious, but when the first LDS missionaries came to their door they rejected the elders and their message.

Sometime later, Neils went with six of his friends to a meeting sponsored by the two foreigners from Utah. But the Danes had no intentions of listening to the elders testify about the restored gospel. They wanted to disrupt the meeting and drive the missionaries and their religion out of Nørager. When they arrived at the meeting, they sat on the front row. Neils, like his companions, kept his hands in his pockets, concealing a rock within each palm.

The first American arose and declared that the gospel of Jesus Christ had been restored through Joseph Smith. After he sat down the other elder spoke, continuing to boldly preach and testify to the truth of the gospel.

On the front row, the seven Danes made no effort to throw their rocks. As the elders spoke, Neils was overwhelmed by the Spirit. He gradually pulled his hands out of his pockets, and tears began to roll down his face.

He knew the doctrines preached by the missionaries were true, and he committed himself to learn more. His wife, daughter, and one son were soon baptized. He and his other two sons joined a few months later.

In 1862 the family immigrated to Utah, settling in the small Danish community of Millville in Cache Valley. Neils set up the community's first blacksmith shop and later was called by President Brigham Young to build a molasses mill to encourage the Saints in the area to plant sorghum.

More than a century later, in July 1984, seventy-two of his descendants converged on the Millville City Park to dedicate a stone monument to Neils Peter Hjorth, a Danish convert who became the first man to build and operate a molasses mill in Cache Valley.

19

He Fulfilled His Goal

When he was about seven, Michael Wolbach told his mother he wanted to become a priest and serve as a missionary in a foreign land. "So much had been given to me in my life, I wanted to give something back," he later recalled.

Eighteen years later, Elder Wolbach boarded a plane bound for Europe, where he fulfilled his goal in a way he had never anticipated. He wasn't a priest but an elder in The Church of Jesus Christ of Latter-day Saints.

Michael still marvels at the series of events leading to his conversion and his mission. He grew up in a religious home, attending church with his family and serving as an altar boy, lector, and youth leader. His parents wanted him to have a secular education before entering the ministry. Michael graduated from a public high school and the University of Vermont before joining a religious order and entering a theological school in Boston, Massachusetts.

"During the time I was there, I made some interesting discoveries that made it difficult to continue," he relates. "Even though they believed in the Bible, there was almost no emphasis on reading the Bible."

The more he studied, the more disillusioned he became. He dropped out in the fall of 1980 after thirteen months. He moved to Florida and began working as a file clerk at the University of Florida. In July 1981 he and his supervisor, Mark Stevens, began talking about religion. Mark said he was a Latter-day Saint and then asked Michael about his religious beliefs. "I said, 'I don't believe the church of Christ exists on this earth.' He asked me what would be my ideal church."

Michael said the true Church would have no paid ministry, would emphasize the family, would have modern revelation, and would believe in preparing for the Millennium. "I know the true church doesn't exist," he said, "because if it did, everyone would be a member."

Mark testified that the true church was on earth and offered to have missionaries meet with Michael and teach him about the restored gospel. He readily agreed to listen, and after hearing the Joseph Smith story, he knew the Church was true. On October 18, 1981, he was baptized.

Two and a half years later he left for a mission to Switzerland and Austria. "Finally," he says, "I felt the fulfillment of the missionary life I had wanted as a youngster."

20

Healed by "Impostors"

Despite the demands of having fourteen children, John Tanner had become a wealthy and influential resident of Bolton, New York, by 1832. But he had also contracted a painful disease that covered his left leg with black sores. He sought out several of the country's top physicians, but each of them said approximately the same thing: "You are beyond the reach of medicine, and I can do you no good."

In September 1832, a notice was circulated that two LDS elders would preach near John's home. He was delighted by the announcement because it was an opportunity to battle "Mormon heresy" and prevent the people from being led astray by these "impostors."

Using a wheelchair-like vehicle, John attended the meeting. As two brothers, Elders Simeon and Jared Carter, preached the restored gospel, a change came over John. Instead of challenging their doctrines, he invited the missionaries to his home so he could learn more. The trio spent the evening talking about the gospel. By 11:00 P.M. John said that he was ready to be baptized—but that he couldn't receive the ordinance.

"Why not?"

"Because of my diseased leg," John answered. "I haven't walked on it in six months."

The elders asked John if he believed the gospel of Jesus Christ anciently had enough power to heal all diseases. John said yes. Then, the brothers questioned, why wouldn't it have the power to heal him now?

"I have never thought about it, but I believe the Lord could heal me," John said.

Elder Jared Carter then arose and commanded him in the name of Jesus Christ to arise and walk.

"I arose, threw down my crutches, and walked the floor praising God," John recalled. He then walked a mile to the place where he was to be baptized.

John Tanner later sold his land and joined the Saints in Kirtland, where he liberally loaned and donated his money to the Church. He was the great-great-grandfather of President N. Eldon Tanner, who was a counselor to four Church Presidents; the father-in-law of Amasa M. Lyman, who served as an additional counselor in the First Presidency in the 1840s; and the grandfather of Elder Francis M. Lyman, a member of the Council of the Twelve.

21

They Kept Their Composure

As a young boy growing up in Italy, Sergio Zicari had two strong desires: "One was to have a family and become a father, and the other was to serve Jesus Christ as a religious minister, but I did not want to do it as a 'profession' but as a volunteer."

When investigating religion through the years, he looked for more than a simple Sunday faith; he wanted a faith that would influence his thoughts and actions seven days a week. "What I searched for was not a religion-like palliative of my doubts and afflictions but a true style of life," he says. He tried to be active in the religion of his parents, but too often came away feeling perplexed and dissatisfied. His church leaders couldn't answer his questions: "What happens to families after this life?" and "What happened to the Church organized by the Savior?" Studying the Bible elicited more questions than answers.

He attended several churches, meeting many people who seemed to be striving to follow Christ. But who was right? Which was the one true church? He became more confused yet continued to attend the church he had grown up in, serving as a youth leader. In 1970, he suggested to the priest that the parish organize a series of conferences for other Christian religions in the church's auditorium. The priest gave his approval, and Sergio contacted several religions, including two LDS missionaries living in a town eighteen miles away. What little Sergio knew about the Mormons was negative, but he still wanted to hear what the missionaries had to say. The conference proved to be the beginning of the gospel being preached in Mestre, Italy.

"During their lecture, the missionaries were insulted and mocked by the ministers from the other religions," Sergio recalls.

"Nevertheless, the missionaries continued to smile and share their testimonies of the truth. The doctrines I heard that evening from the lips of the missionaries did not attract me very much, but their quietness, composure, and serenity were so great that I immediately desired to become like them."

At the end of the conference, Sergio was the only person who wanted to hear more about the Church. While listening to the first lesson, he realized the necessity of having a living prophet. The missionaries also had answers to his difficult questions. "For the first time in my life, I was learning about a church that made me think: 'I would be proud to belong to such a church and to know the people that I have so longed to meet.' I knew I must discover what made them so special, and I must try to become like them."

But there was one obstacle. The missionaries always testified, "I know that . . ." Sergio didn't know; he agreed and could accept some things but couldn't say anything for sure. He continued to listen to the missionaries and attend LDS meetings, but hesitated to commit himself to baptism. In the meantime, the missionaries rented an apartment in Mestre and established a branch there. More than a year later, Sergio was called to teach a class using only the scriptures as a manual. "This was a great challenge to me," Sergio relates. "I never taught and was not able to speak in public, but I sought to be worthy of the trust [the branch president] gave me. Thus I studied the scriptures in greater depth, and I began to correlate them. This helped me to develop a stronger testimony (and that was all I needed) about the Book of Mormon as another testimony of Jesus Christ's work."

Again he asked the missionaries to teach him. This time he was joined by his fiancée, Elisabetta Danesin. "The second time the message was clear to me. As I listened to them speak about the gospel, I felt a special joy within my soul." He was baptized April 22, 1972. Elisabetta also joined the Church. They were later sealed in the temple and have been blessed with children.

Sergio was soon called to serve in the branch presidency. He has since been a branch president, district president, and counselor in both the mission presidency and the Italy Venice Stake. Thus the two great desires he had as a child were fulfilled in the restored gospel. "I have found my pearl of great price."

22

Recruited for Service

In the spring of 1981 Tim Canty was disheartened and becoming desperate. He had been looking for work for nearly five months with no success, and his bills were beginning to mount. At times like these, he had often sought peace and comfort by listening to the Mormon Tabernacle Choir. On this spring day, however, he didn't realize he would hear more than the Choir's music—he would soon listen to its message.

Tim had just turned on the Choir music and lain down when his daughter Andrea interrupted him. "Dad, a couple of guys are coming over to our house."

"What kind of guys?"

"They look like navy recruiters," she said.

Tim got up and looked out the window. Sure enough, two men wearing white shirts, ties, dark pants, and shined shoes were walking across the road toward his house. They did look like navy recruiters, he thought, although they were a bit on the young side. The young men stopped outside Tim's house, turned, and started walking back across the street. Tim shrugged his shoulders and lay back down to listen to the Choir. "I said to myself, 'They're wasting their time; I'm too old for the navy. No prospects here.'"

A few minutes later Andrea returned and said, "They're here." Tim answered the door. The first thing he noticed were the missionaries' name-tags with The Church of Jesus Christ of Latter-day Saints inscribed on them. "We would like to talk to you about the true church," one of the elders said. Tim, a strapping man with a black belt in Judo, answered: "Why do you consider yourselves the true church? I always thought my church was the true church."

After he listened to the missionaries respond, Tim decided to rib the elders a little more. "How is it that Mormons happen to be in this area? I didn't think any Mormons lived east of the Rocky Mountains?" Tim was surprised to hear that a meetinghouse was located nearby. The missionaries set up an appointment to return and teach the Cantys.

Tim had been searching for a religion for many years. He and his wife, Georgia, had attended church in their youth and felt they should pass some religious stability on to their children. But the family bounced from one church to another, never finding answers or gaining a feeling of belonging.

When the missionaries returned to teach him, Tim tried to keep an open mind to what they were saying. "As I heard them talk about the plan of salvation, I got goose bumps all over me," Tim relates. "When told about the preexistence, I was sure I had read that story before in an old Bible at my grandparents' house in South Carolina." (Three years later he would visit his grandparents, dig out the old Bible, but not find any of the information he thought he had seen in there.)

The doctrines taught by the missionaries struck Tim with such forcefulness, he knew from day one they were true. He tried to persuade his wife to sit in on the next lesson, but she refused, "I don't want anything to do with it. If I see the truth in it, I'll recognize it."

However, every time the missionaries came, she rushed upstairs. Tim was furious because he knew if she heard only a portion of what the two young men were saying, she would want to know more. During the missionaries' third visit, they again talked about premortal life and life after death. Tim heard the squeaking of the stairs behind him and knew Georgia was listening. "I said to myself, 'That's a gotcha.' "

"It was like a bell going off in my head," says Georgia about the things she heard that first time. "I decided, 'This is interesting; I want to hear more about what these young men are saying,' I walked downstairs and sat down. You never saw two happier missionaries."

Andrea, who later served a mission, felt equally good about what the missionaries were teaching. The elders invited the family out to church. The Cantys, who are black, had had negative experiences attending other churches, but felt immediately welcome in the Vineland Ward in New Jersey. "I felt like I had come home,"

Tim recalls. On September 17, 1981, Tim was baptized at the stake center—though he was a little disappointed that they didn't serve steak there. He also was surprised to find out that bishopric didn't mean the bishop's name was Rick. Having since served as a bishop of the ward, he tries to ease the transition for new converts.

On October 11, 1981, Georgia and Andrea joined the Church. The family accepted the gospel wholeheartedly, paying a full tithing despite their financial difficulties. Within a short time, Tim received a telephone call from a mining firm he had applied at five months earlier. The company wanted to know if he was still interested in working as an engineer there. Tim learned that the two men in charge of hiring had become ill and hadn't been able to get back with him earlier. He got the job.

Another blessing came in December 1981 when Tim's son, Timothy Canty III, called and asked if Tim would like to be present at his baptism.

"What church did you join?" the father asked.

"The true Church of Jesus Christ of Latter-day Saints," his son said. "What else would I join?"

Tim later asked his son why he had decided to contact the missionaries and investigate the LDS church. "Because of the effect it has had on you," replied the son.

23

Guilty as Charged

The Reverend Albert Potts of the Antioch Baptist Church in Pine Hill, Tennessee, charged J. N. Rice and his wife with "entertaining Mormon elders and advocating their doctrine." He personally delivered the accusation—grounds for being cast out of the church—to the Rices' McDonald, Tennessee, farm late in December 1902.

When Albert Potts confronted Mrs. Rice with the charges, to his surprise she admitted guilt and informed him that she and her husband had been baptized in the restored Church of Jesus Christ. The minister stormed out of the house, refusing to listen to their explanation.

On December 27, 1902, the couple submitted a letter to their former congregation in hopes that it might induce "some honest soul to investigate the faith we have embraced, for 'we are not ashamed of the gospel of Christ, for it is the power of God unto salvation.' "

The letter was read before the congregation by Deck Mitchell, a deacon in the church. When he had finished the reading, he was so incensed at its contents that he tore the letter up and threw it in the flames of the church heater.

In the letter, the Rices said that their daughter, who had died in July, had been investigating the Mormon church for three years, and that before her death she had testified that she knew it to be true.

Two months later, the letter continued, another of their daughters was stricken with a similar disease. Within three months, the disease had reduced her to almost a skeleton. Latter-day Saint elders were called from Chattanooga, Tennessee, to administer to her. Two hours after the blessing, she arose from her bed and helped prepare the evening meal. Some would make light of the healing, the Rices wrote, but devils can do nothing in the name of Jesus Christ.

"We have not apostatized from any of the doctrines of Christ and his Apostles, but we have come to a more perfect understanding and knowledge," the couple wrote. "If there is any one among you who is seeking truth, we invite you to come and see us."

24

An Answer to Prayer

Marjorie Woolcott of Highland, California, had received an answer to her prayers, but at first she refused to admit it.

Elders Jerry Ewell and Joel Hall from the California San Bernardino Mission had visited her home three times during August and September of 1980, and each time she had turned them away. By the time of their third visit she was starting to get interested in who they were. When she found out they were Mormons, she couldn't believe they had come in answer to her prayers. But despite her misgivings, she agreed to read a pamphlet they left.

When Marjorie, a single parent, asked her two daughters about their investigating another religion, they adamantly refused. They had looked into other religions before, only to come away disillusioned.

It wasn't long before family problems again caused Marjorie to turn to the Lord for help. Within half an hour of her offering a prayer, the doorbell rang, and the same two missionaries—who had been impressed to try again—were standing outside the door. "I didn't tell them or the kids about my prayer," Marjorie says. "I just wanted to hear what they had to say."

The Woolcotts were receptive to the message of the restored gospel. They listened to the discussions and asked several questions. Several visits later, the missionaries showed the film "Families are Forever." "I knew what they were saying was true when I saw the film," says Marjorie.

She began to cry. When the elders asked her what was wrong, she told them that each time they had previously come to visit, she had just finished praying, seeking to find out which church was right.

At first she hadn't connected the elders' visits with her prayers. However, after four times she couldn't deny that they had come in answer to her prayers. And as the elders taught her, everything seemed to fall into place. She and her daughters were baptized in November 1980.

25

Green Street Conversion

An older lady sat in a rocking chair listening to the message of Elders John Van Wagoner and David Israel. Although the scene was just a dream, the lady, her rocking chair, and the hardwood floors of her house seemed to Elder Van Wagoner as if they actually existed. As he pondered it, he also recalled a circle-like neighborhood and his persistence in persuading her to listen.

"I got enthused about it and started to think the Lord had a lady he wanted us to find," wrote Elder Van Wagoner of the experience he had in September 1983. He prayed to know whether his "thoughts and ambitions were right." He felt a positive response, so he scanned a map of Keene, New Hampshire, picking out a neighborhood with a circular layout. Later, as he was eating breakfast, the word *green* stood out in his mind. "I got up and walked to the map and began looking down the columns of streets. Right in the center of the column was Green Street."

Finding the street, the elders knocked on about ten doors without any success. Elder Van Wagoner began to wonder whether he had made a mistake.

At the next house, an older lady came to the door. She wasn't as old as he had expected, but seeing her gave him a new surge of confidence. She let them in, but to Elder Van Wagoner's dismay there was no rocking chair or hardwood floor. After teaching the woman a discussion, they left without a return appointment. Elder Van Wagoner began to doubt his feelings, but Elder Israel reassured him.

When Elder Van Wagoner knocked on the next door, no one answered. He felt impressed to knock again, and this time an older lady came to the door. Marian Davis, recently widowed, said she was a member of another church. Elder Van Wagoner asked her to let them share an important message with her.

On the condition that they be brief, she let them in. To Elder Van Wagoner's satisfaction, she sat on an old rocking chair resting on a hardwood floor.

Three weeks later, Marian Davis was baptized.

26

Obeying the Spirit

When thirty-seven-year-old Elder William O'Neill arrived in New Pitsligo, Scotland, in the 1880s, he had no missionary companion or Church members to work with.

In three months' time, two men—John Knox and John Murray—were converted to the Church. Despite his baptism, John Murray continued attending Salvation Army testimony meetings, and Elder O'Neill would occasionally go with him. Near the close of one meeting, the captain asked if any person in the congregation would like to speak a word for Jesus.

"I felt strongly prompted to arise and bear my testimony, but somehow I could not muster up sufficient courage," Elder O'Neill recalled.

He deeply regretted disobeying the Spirit. Just a few years before, he had promised the Lord he would serve Him all the days of his life. This promise had been made while Elder O'Neill was buried under thirty-feet of earth from a mine cave-in.

Up to that time, he had been a "wild, thoughtless young man." But after being rescued he kept his promise to the Lord, and he had been worthy to be called on a mission to Great Britain. Now he resolved never to let an opportunity to bear his testimony pass again, no matter what the consequences. A short time later, Elder O'Neill was joined by Elder Joseph Sharp, who had just arrived from Salt Lake City. Elder O'Neill soon felt impressed that they should attend another Salvation Army meeting.

When the opportunity came to speak, "My whole frame shook, and it seemed as if I would choke," Elder O'Neill recorded. Praying silently for help, he arose and went to the podium. He preached for half an hour about the first principles of the gospel and the Restoration, challenging those interested in the truth to hear the elders.

William Burney, an officer in the Salvation Army, entered the hall that evening and listened to Elder O'Neill. After the service, the elders gave him a book on Church doctrine, and Burney spent most of the night reading it. In the morning he turned in his Salvation Army uniform and requested that his name be taken off their rolls because he was going to join The Church of Jesus Christ of Latter-day Saints.

27

She Needed Answers

Over the years, Raymond and Leah Belle Hawkes of the Sugar City Second Ward, in Sugar City, Idaho, had prepared seven sons for missions and supported them in the mission field. Now it was their turn to serve a mission.

Called to the Ohio Akron Mission in the summer of 1986, the pair settled into an apartment and began serving in the mission office by day and proselyting in the evenings.

After two months in the mission field, Sister Hawkes developed a case of homesickness. She longed for a slice of homemade wheat bread, fresh from the oven. Making bread was something she had been doing for forty years. Having left her baking utensils in Idaho, she had to buy new pans, along with yeast and wheat flour. That evening she made the dough and kneaded it by hand in "Ohio's notorious humidity." By 11:00 P.M. the bread was ready for the oven.

"I could almost taste it," she says. "Then disaster struck. My oven wouldn't work."

Her husband tried to console her. In view of the late hour, he suggested that she freeze the dough to use it another day, but Sister Hawkes was determined to have the bread. She started searching for an oven. Wandering upstairs, she knocked at the apartment of Virginia Jeschke, a neighbor she had met only once.

Virginia Jeschke, a sixty-one-year-old widow, invited the sixty-two-year-old Idaho missionary in and agreed to let her use the oven. "We talked away the time while the delicious fragrance of wheat bread drifted throughout the room," Sister Hawkes recalls. "During those hours, Virginia shared with me her confusion about life hereafter. Her first husband had died in World War II, and her second husband of forty years had died a few months ago. She had some questions she wanted to ask a minister."

President T. Kay Edmunds of the Ohio Akron Mission was coming to the Hawkeses' apartment the next evening, so Sister Hawkes suggested the mission president as someone who could answer the widow's questions. As she and her new friend ate a slice of warm bread, they set up a meeting time.

Virginia met with President Edmunds and then began studying with the elders. Elder and Sister Hawkes sat in on the discussions, providing fellowship to their neighbor, who received baptism in November 1986. About six months later she died, knowing she would be reunited with loved ones on the other side.

III

Teaching by Example

28

Because of Snyder

Charley Company's advance into the jungle near Tay Ninh, South Vietnam, ground to a halt by midmorning April 7, 1967, when the point man ran into a swarm of red ants. As the soldier picked off the ants, Captain Jim Cain, company commander, crawled over to LDS Chaplain Claude Newby and whispered: "Claude, I want you to teach me about the Mormon religion."

Newby was stunned—not because the captain had expressed interest in the Church, but because the officer had broken his strictly enforced rule of not talking about anything but the mission when in combat.

"I'll be glad to, Jim, but why now?" Newby asked.

"Because of Bill Snyder. He's the most cheerful, dependable, hard-working, and courageous soldier I've ever known. I want to know about a religion that makes a young man like that."

The next time the company stopped, it was at a ditch filled with freshly dug enemy positions, a sure sign that a fight was close at hand. There the men of Charley Company waited while American jets pounded enemy positions in front of them.

When the company started moving again, Chaplain Newby walked past Bill Snyder's machine gun squad. "Chaplain Newby," said the returned missionary from Mapleton, Utah, "don't look so sad. It hasn't rained yet, and it may not even rain bullets today."

Less than a minute later, machine-gun fire from about a hundred feet in front of the column killed the point man and wounded several others. Chaplain Newby dived for cover between two waist-high termite hills, but found himself still in the machine gun's line of fire. He turned his head just as bullets chopped off a bush touching his neck. The next burst hit in front of his head, filling his face with dirt. Snyder ran up behind one of the termite hills. He hesitated when he got to Chaplain Newby and looked at him "like he knew what was going to happen." Then he sprinted twenty feet forward, dived to the ground, and fired his machine gun into the enemy position. The enemy gunner's next burst killed Bill Snyder, but it allowed Chaplain Newby and the other men to scramble to safety.

A few months after Bill Snyder's death, a soldier from Charley Company told Chaplain Newby he had quit smoking. "Why are you telling me?" the chaplain asked. "I didn't tell you to quit smoking."

"I know," said the soldier, "but Snyder did."

29

The "Chance" Meeting

Their four daughters were getting older, and Thomas and Doris Montoya of Auburndale, Florida, wanted to take one last family vacation before the girls moved on to college and marriage. So in 1974 the family loaded up their four-wheel-drive vehicle and utility trailer with camping gear and headed west to explore "the back country, we knew not where."

By Wednesday of the second week, they were in central Utah at Natural Bridges National Monument. At a place called Bears Ears, they took a gravel road into the mountains of the Manti-La Sal National Forest. They soon spotted six four-wheel-drive vehicles stopped at an intersection. Montoya asked if the group knew of any campsites nearby. One of the men in the group, Russell M. Billings, a dentist from Provo, Utah, suggested the Montoyas join their group. "We're just a bunch of Provo Mormons out having a good time for a few days," Billings said.

The Florida family spent three "marvelous" days with the group, visiting old Indian ruins and scenic vistas. "It was truly an answer to a silent prayer I had that someone local who knew the back country would take us in tow and show us around," Thomas says. The Montoyas also were impressed with the way the Latter-day Saints treated them and each other. "We recognized that there was something special about them that we wanted. Those few days were the highlight of our vacation."

When the Montoyas returned to Florida, they checked out from the library several books on Mormons. "We wanted to be a part of it," they explained. Thomas contacted an LDS friend, who referred the missionaries to the family. After being taught the gospel, the parents and the youngest daughter were baptized on

March 7, 1975. Three weeks later another daughter was baptized, and within four years the two oldest also had joined the Church. Twelve years after his baptism, Thomas was sustained as first counselor in the Lakeland Florida Stake Presidency.

"Our lives have been richly blessed through the gospel, and I often think of that 'chance' meeting in the mountains," Thomas reminisces. "Ten minutes either way and we would not have met the Mormons. I know that meeting was the work of our Heavenly Father."

30

I Can't Figure You Out

The new marine, Harlow Cheney, was tall and athletically built, but that wasn't what made him stand out from the other men in his platoon in 1944.

He was reserved, calm, and self-disciplined. He spent a lot of time meditating and reading the scriptures. The other marines indulged in drinking and partying, but Harlow rejected offers to join them. He didn't drink or smoke. Harlow's behavior puzzled Clifford Chebahtah, a burly Indian sergeant from the state of Oklahoma. One day while Harlow sat alone whittling on a stick, he was approached by the sergeant. "Cheney, I can't figure you out," Clifford said. "You don't do any of the things the other men do. You're all by yourself. You're just different. Where do you come from and why do you act this way?"

Harlow related that he was from Idaho and didn't do a lot of those things because his religion taught against it.

"Idaho," replied Clifford. "Don't tell me you're one of those Utah and Idaho Mormons!"

"Yep," Harlow said.

Clifford continued to watch the young Idahoan. He often asked Harlow about Mormonism. After some discussion, the Idahoan offered his sergeant a copy of the Book of Mormon, saying, "You ought to read this; it's about your ancestors."

Clifford turned down the Book of Mormon. He began wondering if this deeply religious soldier would be able to fire his rifle to kill another human being. In the heat of the battle, could he depend on the Mormon marine? Their company was headed for Japan's heavily fortified Pacific atoll of Iwo Jima. It was to be one of the bloodiest battles of World War II. Clifford voiced his fears to the unassuming Idahoan. Harlow told the sergeant he didn't need to worry. "I'll be with you, and I'll do all that is expected of me."

The night before the landing at Iwo Jima, Clifford retired deep into the ship to a place where he was sure he could be alone. He laid his weapons of war aside, then knelt down and prayed. He said that if the Lord spared his life, he would serve Him in any way he could. When Clifford's men hit the beach the next morning at Iwo Jima, they suffered heavy losses. After a few hours, most of the marines in Clifford's unit lay dead. Only five, including Harlow, had survived the initial battle, and all of them were wounded. They were evacuated to different hospitals, and Clifford would never see Harlow again.

Clifford returned to the United States, married, and settled in Anadarko, Oklahoma. He forgot about Harlow Cheney. In fact, he recalled his first name as Ralph, not Harlow Cheney. Then one night after he came home from work his wife told him to get dressed up because they were going to have company. Two LDS missionaries visited and taught his family the gospel. After he listened to their first discussion, he didn't want them to leave. He pleaded for them to stay "and tell me more." His family was baptized on July 3, 1949, along with thirty-five other people at a service attended by Elder Spencer W. Kimball, then an Apostle.

During the years before his death in January 1986, he longed to find Harlow Cheney and thank him for his example. But all efforts to find the missionary marine failed. However, when Delos and Verla Lusk returned to Sugar City, Idaho, from a mission to Oklahoma, they resumed the search for "Ralph" Cheney. They had about given up—especially after Clifford's death—but something kept them looking. Finally, while visiting with friends from Paul, Idaho, they looked at an alphabetical listing of the 27th Marine Battalion Replacement and found Harlow Cheney's name listed two lines below Clifford Chebahtah. Their friends were shocked. They knew a Harlow Cheney who lived only fifteen miles away in Heyburn, Idaho. The Lusks called Harlow and set up an appointment to meet him.

The first thing the Lusks asked him was if he remembered Clifford Chebahtah. He did. They then told him that Clifford and his family had joined the Church. It may have taken a few years, but the old sergeant had figured out why Harlow had been different, and in the meantime, learned a little bit about his ancestors too.

31

I'm a Mormon Boy

In 1943, twenty-five-year-old Vaha'i Tonga, a recent graduate of the government school, Tonga College, was offered an assignment as principal and director of education on a northern Tongan island known as "Tin Can." "We'll call the Mormon boy, because he's dependable," a college official had said. But Vaha'i was reluctant to go because no Church members lived on the island.

When he had first enrolled in Tonga College, he was the only Latter-day Saint in the school. But he wasn't ashamed to say, "I'm a Mormon boy. I haven't tasted a cigarette, and I haven't tasted liquor."

Some of the other students poked fun at him when he prayed each night. His closest roommate in the large sleeping room would stand next to him as he prayed and say, "Look and listen. Here is Joseph Smith. He's praying now." But within two weeks, that roommate began joining him in prayer. "Quiet. Vaha'i Tonga is praying," he now yelled. Later, all the boys in the room began to gather for "family prayer." Many subsequently joined the Church.

Despite his missionary success at the school, however, Vaha'i had no desire to take his wife to Tin Can. Before he could refuse the assignment, however, the mission president came to him and said, "Brother Tonga, the Lord has called you to go on a mission to Tin Can Island." So Vaha'i went, with advice from his mission president to wait three months before trying to talk about the Church. This would avoid trouble with the government.

But two former college roommates living on the island had different ideas. They had been telling local people that Vaha'i was a Mormon missionary. "If you want to listen," they said, "he's got a really fantastic Church."

The night after he arrived, Vaha'i held his first cottage meeting. He soon learned about an inactive member who had become an important man in another religion. The man had prepared the way for missionary work by teaching principles of the restored gospel in the other church. "Because of him, it was easier for me to preach the gospel," Vaha'i recalls.

In a month he had baptized five people and organized a Sunday School. Within three years, seven missionaries had been assigned to the thirty-four-member branch on the island.

32

Example Opened the Door

In January 1954, George and Truena Love were surprised to receive a phone call from two sister missionaries who said they were at the bus station in Ruston, Louisiana. The Loves, Ruston's only LDS family, invited Sister Leta E. Bartholomew and her companion to their home and helped them search for an apartment.

The sisters searched and searched, but with little more than one hundred dollars a month to live on the pair found most lodgings too expensive. Finally one lady referred them to the Tutens, an older couple who had rented in the past.

When Edgar L. Tuten, Jr., answered the door, the sisters introduced themselves as missionaries from The Church of Jesus Christ of Latter-day Saints. Edgar said that he thought what they were doing was commendable but that he wasn't interested in renting out the apartment. He then asked where the sisters were from. When they said Utah and Idaho, he exclaimed, "Utah! That's where the *Mormons* are."

The sisters said they were Mormon missionaries, and Edgar promptly invited them into his house. After some discussion, he asked if Ezra Taft Benson, then Secretary of Agriculture, was a member of their Church. They answered, "He is one of our Church's Twelve Apostles."

"Yes," Edgar said with a smile. "I know. He's a good man, and I like him. I admire him for what he's doing. He believes in something, and he's sticking to it. He has integrity and honesty. He's doing what he thinks is right."

After a brief pause, Edgar said he still didn't want to rent the apartment, but if the missionaries were interested they could stay in the apartment free. "Anyone who's a member of the same church as Ezra Taft Benson is welcome to these rooms, and we're proud to have you," he said.

"The apartment was one of the cleanest and nicest places in which I lived as a missionary," Sister Bartholomew remembers. "It was centrally located, and, best of all, it was owned by our landlords and friends, the Tutens."

Before the sisters left Ruston, they taught the Tutens the gospel and left them a Book of Mormon. "As we waved good-bye, each wiping a tear or two from our faces," Sister Bartholomew relates, "I remembered how this special friendship had begun, and how two missionary sisters had been blessed with a clean, comfortable, well-located apartment—because of the righteous influence of President Benson on a man he never met."

33

You Saved One Today

During the Vietnam conflict, Charles L.A. Jeffery was part of a helicopter rescue unit that picked up fighter pilots shot down in action. For a time, Charles was paired with a young, talented pilot he remembers only as Captain Hanks. Being an enlisted man, Charles didn't see much of Hanks outside of duty, but on several occasions the two men ate breakfast together.

Before getting aboard the helicopter to go on standby, Charles remembers that the last words the captain would always say to him were "Well, Sarge, I wonder if we will save anyone today." In the weeks and months they flew together, the pair rescued several downed pilots, some under difficult and dangerous circumstances.

"In these different situations, I noted that Captain Hanks not only had outstanding qualities in his military duties, but also had these same qualities when dealing with people," Charles remembers. "He had a Christian way about him. Even when times were very dangerous, Captain Hanks had a light in his eye that seemed to tell others all would be OK. He seemed to know where he was going should anything go wrong."

Charles recalls one instance where they were flying in to pick up a downed pilot and started drawing fire. "Of course, under those circumstances most people would be yelling, screaming, and shouting out orders. But Captain Hanks seemed to have everything under control as he gave out orders. I've been in a lot of combat situations, and you could tell that the guy in charge was just as scared as you were. If there was somebody who didn't seem scared, it was Captain Hanks."

The captain was transferred to another unit as a fighter aircraft pilot, while Charles was assigned to another helicopter with new crew members and a new aircraft commander. One afternoon, months later, Charles's helicopter was called out to rescue a pilot whose jet had been shot down. "We saw the pilot lying on the ground, motionless in an open area," he says. "As the helicopter came closer I jumped to the ground and went to him."

It was Captain Hanks.

Charles yelled for the medics to help the captain. The pilot looked up at his friend and "with that light still in his eye, said, 'Well, Sarge, you saved one today.' "

Those were the last words Captain Hanks ever said. "If you pick up a man, and he dies in your arms, you don't forget that," Charles explains. "We just knew that he was LDS. Since then, I have associated exemplary life with that of Captain Hanks and LDS."

Charles retired from the military in 1972 and eventually settled in Utah. As the years passed, he often wondered what Captain Hanks knew about life that he didn't. In the early 1980s he investigated the Church and was baptized. "As I reflect on previous contacts I had with the Church and its members, I find that the life of Captain Hanks stands out in my memory. Our crew was not able to save Captain Hanks, but he helped save me—spiritually."

He Felt at Home

While attending the priesthood session of general conference in April 1986, Mark Lerohl was impressed by President Ezra Taft Benson's call for every worthy young man to fulfill a mission. "The prophet said that education can wait, marriage can wait, and blessings await him who serves," Mark recalls. "This statement struck me strongly."

That night in his apartment, he prayed to learn if he should serve a mission. The answer was an emotional, "overpowering" yes.

Mark had been a member of the Church for only a year, and previously he had attended several churches. As he was growing up in Minnetonka, Minnesota, he was active in a denomination that had played a major role in his family's heritage for several generations.

"As I grew older, I realized many of the doctrines didn't make sense to me and contradicted what I believed deep inside," Mark says. "This is when I decided that there was more to religion than just plain old traditions, and I started looking into other churches."

After high school, Mark attended Southwest Missouri State University in Springfield. One day his roommate who belonged to a fundamentalist denomination quizzed Mark about what his church believed. "In God, I guess," Mark responded. "I never really gave it much thought." The roommate began telling Mark about his beliefs, backing up his statements with Bible scriptures. Mark was impressed and attended the roommate's church. "As I sat in this two-thousand-seat congregation, I felt the excitement of the members and the enthusiasm of the preacher and the deacons," Mark recalls. He also agreed with many of the doctrines espoused by the fundamentalists, but he rejected some of their other beliefs. He accepted baptism, while still harboring the feeling that something was lacking.

The more involved in the religion he became, the more questions about doctrine arose in his mind. When he couldn't get answers to these questions, he became frustrated and dropped out of church. He began to enjoy the social side of college life. At the end of his freshman year, he transferred to the University of Wisconsin in Eau Claire. He couldn't explain why he had picked that university, except that he liked the brochures.

He soon made many new friends and again pushed aside his interest in religion while enjoying the university's social scene. All this changed when he met Paul Forcier in the school choir. He now believes he "was sent" to the University of Wisconsin to meet Paul. When Mark first saw Paul, he thought he knew him from somewhere. They gradually became close friends. "I really liked the way he presented himself, and something about him impressed me," Mark recalls.

One day they talked religion. Mark recounted his experiences and frustration in trying to find the right church. When he finished, he listened as Paul mentioned that he was a Mormon. That perked Mark's interest immediately because Mark had never had any contact with Mormons before. He showered Paul with questions and was fascinated by the answers. His curiosity piqued, Mark asked Paul to take him to a Church meeting. Paul eagerly agreed.

"I'll never forget how excited and nervous I was," Mark says. "As I entered the building, I felt a sense of love and peace. The people of the ward were so loving and welcoming that day. I thought, 'These people don't know me from Adam! Yet they treat me as if they've known me my whole life.' "

This never-before-experienced feeling of "home" brought tears of joy to his eyes. He wanted to know more and began studying with the missionaries. When the discussion focused on the Restoration, Mark ran into a snag. "I didn't know how to take the Joseph Smith story. But as I began to read the Book of Mormon and pray, that testimony of the truthfulness of these things came forth, and I was excited to learn more."

Another obstacle sprung up when the missionaries invited him to be baptized. What would Mark's parents and relatives think? He spent hours on his knees, praying his family would understand. They did. "My parents are impressed that a church can influence a young man so much as to have him give up smoking, drinking, and the other things that are so influential to young people."

Paul, who sat in on every missionary discussion, baptized Mark on April 26, 1985. Heeding President Benson's counsel, Mark served in the California Anaheim Mission. "I love this Church with all my heart, and I am so thankful for the gospel that has been restored to the earth in these latter days. It changes lives for the better. I know. I am a product of that change."

35

The Road to Damascus

Paa-Bekoe Welbeck came to the United States with his father in the early 1960s carrying a suitcase and less than a hundred dollars.

He wanted to be a minister, and he soon began working toward that goal at a small liberal arts college in the South. "For four years, I had a chance to live in close contact with ministers in training," he says. "I spoke in many churches. During that time I saw things that frightened me. I thought, 'If this is what Christianity is all about, I don't want to be a part of it.' "

For more than a decade, while he earned a Ph.D. and developed a master plan for becoming a millionaire, he put religion behind him. But then things fell apart, and he almost lost everything. Bitter and angry, he again turned to the Lord. "My heart became contrite. I was begging for new direction in life."

In 1982, one of his regular customers invited him to attend an LDS church service. He didn't know anything about the Church except what he had read in magazines. But he remembered a Latter-day Saint he had met at Boston University in the late 1960s. "I never forgot his face, his manners, and the way he stood out among us—and there were 125 of us from all over the country and the world."

He attended church and received a pamphlet entitled "The Plan of Salvation." It answered questions he had thought nobody could answer. Then he learned about the Joseph Smith story.

"The First Vision did something to me I can't describe—it challenged my intellect." He compared what he had read with the New Testament. Paul's vision on the road to Damascus had always fascinated him, and now he found a correlation between it and Joseph Smith's experience. "I thought, 'If I could accept Paul's vision, why could I not accept Joseph Smith's?' " He stubbornly tried to dismiss this rationale, but he couldn't get Joseph Smith's testimony out of his mind.

"Why would a man put himself through such suffering just to tell a story? What would Joseph Smith have to gain by making up a wild story? Why would the pioneers sacrifice everything to follow a lie? It didn't make any sense."

He went to the bishop in the Kensington, Virginia, ward he had been attending. The bishop's wisdom and sincerity touched him and helped him break some long-held habits without withdrawal symptoms. His baptism marked the end of his "road to Damascus" and the beginning of the "best part" of his life. "I had found what I was looking for when I first came to this country. After seventeen years of wandering, I've come home."

36

Her Bias Became Belief

Margaret R. "Peggy" Levitt says that if she had ever had a prejudice it was against Mormons. "Whenever I heard the word *Mormon*, the hair on the back of my head would bristle. I pictured LDS women as submissive, doing whatever they were told. I didn't perceive them as creative and independent."

Then in 1978, a Latter-day Saint, Bruce Alder, was appointed superintendent of the Southern Nevada Children's Home in Boulder, Nevada, where she worked as a social worker. She noticed something different about Bruce. "He was the best boss I had ever had," she notes. "And you couldn't help but like him."

Soon after moving to Boulder City, Bruce was called as bishop. He invited Peggy to attend church when he was sustained. She was flattered. "I began asking him hundreds of questions about the Church," she recalls. "As he gave me answers, I would shake my head in unbelief and say, 'You can't believe that!' "

But the amount of time Bruce devoted to the Church without getting paid impressed her. She began scrutinizing him and his family. "Of course, I just loved his wife and children. His wife was a housewife, and the number of things she accomplished just amazed me."

Nearly three years after she met Bruce, she purchased a copy of *Gospel Principles* at an LDS bookstore. "I was afraid to tell Bruce that I was looking into his church, and I didn't tell my family or any of my friends because I had been so vocally anti-Mormon that I was kind of embarrassed."

Though the doctrines and the Church meetings struck her as being strange, she continued to study and attended a ward in nearby Las Vegas. The bishop of the Las Vegas ward sent the missionaries to her home. She called herself "a tough case," but neither she nor the missionaries gave up. In September 1981 she was baptized, despite opposition from friends and family.

"I love the Church," says Peggy, who replaced Bruce as superintendent when he was transferred. "It has brought so many things into my life. I've played in basketball tournaments, acted in a play, and taught classes. I had never taught before I joined the Church. The Church has stretched me in a way I hadn't believed possible."

37

Peace Shone in Her Eyes

Paul H. Risk was reared in one religion by parents who were members of another faith. "I think my parents probably were searching and weren't completely satisfied," he recalls. "We attended a number of churches in my youth."

Some of the principles his parents taught him were closely related to the truths he would later learn as a member of the Church. For example, they believed that man came to earth for a purpose, that God could still communicate with man, and that inspiration was critical for man's progress. "Although I am sure they had no real comprehension of how it would be accomplished, my parents believed that families would be reunited in the eternities." At the age of fifteen, he found the latter belief to be especially meaningful when his mother died. Two years later he also lost his father. He was an only child and at the time was living in California. What relatives he had resided half way across the country in Indiana.

"I was alone," he relates.

He enrolled at Pasadena City College in Pasadena, California, where he met Rosalie Robison in a ballroom dance class. "The thing that attracted me to her was an inward peace and tranquility that seemed to shine through her eyes," he says. "It was very apparent that she had sensitivities and feelings that others didn't have, and it was visible in her countenance."

They began dating and soon were discussing religion. When Paul expressed his belief that he would be reunited with his parents in the eternities, "she very pointedly and tactfully said she wished it [exaltation] was as readily obtainable as I thought it was, but it wasn't. She said a person needed to be married under the right circumstances, in the right place, by a person with authority."

Her words stunned him, but he remained skeptical about the things she had told him. She invited him to attend church with her. However, he said, "No thanks," because he didn't feel that he could live the high standards and good life expected of Mormons. But she persisted. "You know that wouldn't be a tremendously different life-style for you because you would make a tremendous Mormon." Paul laughed out loud. Inside, however, he was flattered. He began to look at himself and wonder what would cause her to say that. He began to study with the missionaries.

"I remember thinking, 'This is all well and good, but I don't believe it.' I was waiting for a revelation, a burning in the bosom, and didn't recognize that the feeling of warmth I experienced with the missionaries and at church was the confirmation I was seeking."

He joined the Church in 1958, hoping it was the true church. Later, he and Rosalie were sealed in the temple and performed the temple work for his parents. But it wasn't until ten years after his baptism that his hope was replaced by belief and knowledge.

At that time Paul was a park ranger. He felt a kinship with the outdoors. One evening he went to a mountain above Altadena, California, determined to know if the Book of Mormon really was true. His fervent prayer was answered: "I was filled with an awe-inspiring, glowing warmth, and somewhere in my mind came the phrase 'Read it and you will know.' I did so and was rewarded with the knowledge I sought."

As a forestry scientist, he says there is almost nothing about which he can say "I know," with absolute certainty. But, he adds, "I do know two things: I married the right woman, and I joined the right church."

IV

Member Missionaries

38

Preaching All the Time

In 1969 Jerry Ainsworth started an Institute of Religion class at Virginia Tech University in Blacksburg, Virginia, with only one student. They set a goal to each bring a person into the Church. Four years later, the chain of conversions they had started had resulted in nearly fifty baptisms.

Jerry was a thirty-two-year-old health sciences professor beginning his first year at Virginia Tech. He had organized institute programs before, but chances for success here looked dim. Only one Latter-day Saint, a coed, attended the university. However, within a few months, she brought a friend to institute, and then Jerry did. A short time later, in one of his classes, Jerry corrected a student who had misquoted a Bible scripture. After class, two girls came to talk to him about the scripture. Both students began studying about the Church and were converted.

The following year his institute class members committed to double their numbers. "It was kind of like a mandate," Jerry says. "You didn't feel comfortable attending institute unless you brought an investigator. So every night there were two or three. We had fifteen students at the end of the second year and a little more than thirty after the third year. About fifty students came through the program in four years."

One of these was Charlie Bruington. "It was like a snowball rolling downhill," remembers Charlie. "We were preaching all the time. We could talk to someone and, right after, the Crusaders for Christ were on them, handing out anti-Mormon literature. Talk about the refiner's fire—those who came through were strong; others were too afraid to talk to us."

Charlie was introduced to the gospel in early September 1971. He had swapped dorm rooms with a friend and moved in just before the start of fall quarter at Virginia Tech. Two days later, he wandered down the hall, stopped at the door of Michael Oddenino's room and looked inside. On Michael's shelf, Charlie saw a Bible and a copy of *Jesus the Christ*.

"You must be a Christian?" Charlie noted.

"Yes, I'm a member of The Church of Jesus Christ of Latter-day Saints," replied Michael, a convert of six months.

"I examine all churches," said Charlie, who had never met a Mormon before. "What do you believe?"

"We believe in a living prophet and a restored gospel — with twelve living Apostles and continual revelation. We're not Protestant or Catholic, and we believe in additional scriptures along with the Bible."

"Why, that's either the truth or the biggest farce I've ever heard," Charlie declared.

Michael gave several pamphlets and a copy of the Book of Mormon to his curious visitor. Charlie devoured each one, finding the doctrines to be surprisingly similar to what he had believed for some time. Several months earlier, Charlie had given up on organized religion. He walked out of church after a preacher talked about putting in a new air conditioning unit. The concept of a paid ministry had always sickened him. He deposited his tithing money in the bank and said, "Lord, when I find a place for it, I'll put it in, but until then I'll just call myself a Christian."

Michael invited Charlie to a meeting at the Blacksburg Ward. The building was small, and the congregation sat on folding chairs. But the wonderful spirit for which Charlie had long thirsted filled the chapel. After that, he never missed a meeting. His heart became consumed with the desire to know the Church was true. When he started attending institute classes, he discovered many others who also were seriously investigating the Church. "I was praying up a storm," Charlie recalls. "Meanwhile, all around me others in this core of investigators were getting testimonies and getting ready to join the Church." Finally, a missionary said, "Charlie, you already know it's true." After receiving permission from his parents, he was baptized. Later he served as bishop of the Richmond Second Ward in Richmond, Virginia.

One of those introduced to the gospel by Charlie was David Pohlig, a high school friend and fellow ham radio operator. David had switched dorms for winter quarter 1972 and was trying out a new cafeteria when he saw Charlie sitting in the back of the dining room. "The first thing Charlie told me was 'Dave, I joined the Mormon church last week. Why don't you go to Sunday School with me tomorrow?' " Dave wasn't looking for a new religion. He was proud of his family's heritage and prominence in the Lutheran Church. His brother was a minister. But he couldn't resist Charlie's invitation.

"I thought, 'I'll go along and humor him and then show him where he went wrong,' " Dave relates. "The first class was on the three degrees of glory. Boy, was I ever freaked out. I had been well-versed in Lutheran doctrine. I went to a Lutheran grade school. I knew the Bible better than most Latter-day Saints in the area. But that class blew my mind."

David kept going back, attending activities and meetings. "There was definitely a magnetism there," he says. "One side of you is saying this is nice while the other side of you is saying this is not true. You might say, 'Why did I do all this?' I don't know why. I thought the people were friendly, but doctrinally these people were out to lunch."

After taking the missionary discussions, David began hoping that what he was learning was true. His testimony grew as a result of a series of little events that touched his heart. Soon Charlie baptized him.

David believes what happened that year in the Blacksburg Ward has not been duplicated since. "There was such a camaraderie among the people. Keith Dehonge was president of the LDS [Student Association], and he wasn't even a member. He couldn't join because his father refused to give permission."

David soon accepted the ward's missionary mandate. He gave a copy of the Book of Mormon to Jeanie Redd, who had caught a ride with him to Richmond. A year later she was baptized. He also helped in the conversion of Katherine Davis, who later became his wife.

Jerry Ainsworth moved on, but he still marvels at the missionary spirit that brought so many into the gospel. "It was one of those unique experiences that happens once in a lifetime."

A Date to Teach By

In the October 1984 general conference, a year before he was called to the Council of the Twelve, Elder M. Russell Ballard challenged members to exercise faith and set a date on which to have a person ready to be taught the gospel.

"Do not worry that you do not have someone already in mind," said Elder Ballard, then a member of the Presidency of the First Quorum of the Seventy. "Let the Lord help you as you pray diligently for guidance. Fast and pray, seeking guidance and direction from our Heavenly Father." He said he expected members to be successful and asked them to share their experiences with the Church's missionary department. In the October 1986 conference, he reiterated his challenge. Several members responded. Here are extracts from two of those letters:

Judy L. Stoeltzing of Sacramento, California, wrote that she had picked December 15, 1984, because it was the fifteenth anniversary of her baptism.

"It wasn't long after conference that our son, Casey, told me that his friend, Art, was asking questions about the Church after taking a girl in our ward to a high school homecoming dance. Some of his friends had predicted a boring evening with no drinking, but Art admitted that he had never had a better time. He also wanted to know why Casey always seemed so happy and content with life."

The Stoeltzings invited Art to their home, where the missionaries began teaching him. Art was baptized December 13, 1984, and has since served as a missionary in the Japan Kobe Mission.

From Portland, Oregon, Eugene Hill wrote that he had set December 30, 1987, as his date and had prayed for someone with whom he could share the gospel. Early in December, the full-time missionaries called and asked if he remembered Clarence Lucas, a non-member Eugene had worked with for two years as a stake missionary and for seven years as a home teacher to Clarence's member wife.

"When he expressed to the missionaries in December his desire to join the Church, he said he wouldn't commit anything to anyone but me," Brother Hill relates. "Later, the ward mission leader called and asked if I would go with him to visit Clarence Lucas on the next Tuesday. I went, and Lucas made a firm commitment to be baptized. That evening was December 30, 1987."

Clarence Lucas, then eighty-three, was baptized March 14, 1988.

The Greatest Feeling Ever

On a spring evening in 1976, Garry Bryant lay down to sleep hoping he wouldn't wake up in the morning. Garry, a combat photographer, was nearing the end of his four-year stint in the U.S. Air Force. When he signed up in 1972, he had expected orders to Vietnam, but the United States began pulling out of that conflict, and Garry was shipped to Austin, Texas. He may have been better off in Vietnam.

In Austin, he indulged in a destructive life-style that sapped his spirit and his health. Now he felt surrounded by darkness and just wanted to end it all. "That night I decided I would pray. I said to God, 'All right if you really love us the way you say you do, you won't let me wake up in the morning.' "

When the sun broke through his window the next morning, Garry exploded in anger. He was still alive. But his prayer had been answered; the Lord just needed time to prepare his heart.

Garry had been reared by his grandparents who were devout members of a religion with strict rules of conduct. Some of these rules, when combined with the church's doctrines, struck him as contradictory. "They taught very strongly that you didn't exist before you were born," he recalls. "When you died—that was it; you were dead. There was no spirit. There was no intelligence. I was taught this all through school and at church. But I never believed it. Inside I had this innate belief that I had existed before this life, that there was a spirit within me, and that when I died, I would continue to live."

In high school Garry rebelled, declaring himself an agnostic with no belief in God. This freed his conscience and allowed him to live by his own standards, which were to eat, drink, and be merry as long as it "didn't hurt anybody." Bad habits became addictions, and Garry's life was headed downward. Joining the Air Force slowed his downward spiral temporarily, but he soon returned to the dangerous life-style that ultimately caused him to plea for his life to end.

In 1976 he received a letter from old friends John and Shelley Drebenstedt. John related how he had joined the LDS Church, and Shelley had been activated. He told Garry to check out the Latter-day Saints in Austin. "I thought, 'Oh no, my best friends have become religious freaks!' So I wrote them off as my best friends."

Garry wrote back and said thanks but no thanks. The letter marked a turning point, however, because Garry's life began changing—albeit subtly. According to family tradition, Garry was part Sioux Indian. Out of curiosity, he began to investigate the religious traditions of the plains Indians. As he studied, he began remembering the religious teachings of his childhood and was impressed by the common thread of goodness taught in religion. He decided God lived, but his name could be Christ, Buddha, or any other divine personage.

One question he couldn't find the answer to in his religious study was "What is the purpose of life?" Meanwhile, his research into religion hadn't stifled partying. This dark side of his life almost overwhelmed him, but every time he considered delving deeper into drugs, he would hear a little voice inside saying, "No, you're too close to being discharged. Wait until you get out to make your decisions."

When Garry was discharged, he felt a strong desire to go home to Boulder, Colorado. He fought the feeling because he was just breaking into the prominent inner circle of the Austin social scene. But the feeling won out, so he packed his bags and headed home. After he arrived home, he received an invitation from his old friends, the Drebenstedt's, to come to dinner at their home in Westminster, Colorado. Garry accepted.

"What was really eating at me was that I knew they were living the way life should be lived, and I was living in a bad, fast lane."

Garry expected John and Shelley Drebenstedt to preach to him, so he resolved to sit, smile, and nod his head. In a couple of hours it'll be over, he thought. His friends didn't want to preach to Garry, but they did hope to have an opportunity to share the gospel with him. As they prayed about it, they felt that they would know whether he was ready to listen or not.

When John and Shelley opened the door and saw Garry grinning, they knew he was ready. After dinner, the conversation shifted to religion. "They were inspired and directed," Garry recalls. "They talked about where we came from, why we are here, and where we are going—all the stuff I was seeking. I just ate it up. By the end of the conversation, I said, 'I feel like these are things I have always known, and deep inside felt were true.' "

For the next two weeks, Garry took the missionary discussions. He wasn't impressed with the elders, their white shirts, short hair, and naivete, but he continued to study because of his friendship with the Drebenstedts. Then something happened when he attended his first LDS service, a fast and testimony meeting.

"It was really weird seeing people stand up and cry, but there was something happening inside me. I felt the spirit get stronger and stronger. I thought I was having a [drug-induced] flashback. I turned to Shelley and said, 'Shelley, I'm as high as a kite. I'm higher than I have ever been in my entire life.' "

She told him it was the Holy Ghost. The harder he fought the feeling, the stronger it became. Garry thought to himself, "Why are you bucking it; this is the greatest feeling you have ever had in your life."

Another experience causing him to look more seriously at what he was learning occurred after being taught about the commandments. He went with some old drinking buddies to a party. "I looked around at all these guys and thought, 'These aren't my friends. They couldn't care less if I lived or died. As long as I have money, they will be here. But if I'm down on my luck, they won't be here.'

"Then I had a terrible feeling that I was doing something wrong," Garry continues. "I slapped myself across the face and said, 'These guys in the white shirts are really starting to get to you.' "

At the next lesson, the missionaries challenged Garry to be baptized. He just laughed. The elders persisted, and Garry finally agreed to prepare for baptism on a certain date. A few days later, he woke up realizing the date was only a week away. Before that day, he felt he had to know if what the missionaries were telling him was true. "I really started hitting my knees and reading," he says. "A couple of days later, it just hit me: 'Garry you have always wanted a second chance to start life over—this is your chance. If it doesn't work out, you can bag it.' "

That evening when Garry met the missionaries, he had replaced his rebelliousness and cynicism with meekness and sincerity. He stunned the missionaries by saying, "O.K. guys, let's do it." Garry was baptized September 25, 1976. Fifteen months later, at age twenty-three, he entered the mission field, where he was known as the patriarch because of his age and knowledge of the Old Testament.

"In the years I've been a member, whenever I have encountered rocky roads or hard times in school or in my career, I think back to that day in the chapel—the first time the Spirit spoke to me."

Prayer Brings the Gospel

Large apartment buildings lined both sides of a narrow, winding street in Vienna, Austria's Tenth District. To Elders Douglas Smith and Stewart Geary in 1982, this tree-lined thoroughfare was all too familiar. They had hiked along the street to the top of a hill, planning to knock on doors on the way back to their car. But it turned out to be a street they had recently proselyted. "We hated to waste time going and looking for another place to work," recalls Elder Smith.

As they walked down the hill, Elder Smith started running. "I just ran across the street for no reason at all," he recalls. "I ran about fifty yards down the road and cut behind an apartment building."

When Elder Geary caught up with him, Elder Smith was talking to a lady over the building's intercom. The lady, a grandmother, said someone in her apartment might be interested.

That someone was Laura Q. Del Rosario, vice consul for the Philippine Embassy. She was a former missionary for another church who felt something was missing in her life. Since arriving in Austria, she had been praying for help.

Elder Smith was soon transferred, but Elders Stewart Geary and Jay Kemble began teaching the family. The Del Rosarios were receptive and soon started attending church. However, four months later when Elder Smith was transferred back into the area, the family still hadn't been baptized.

Sister Del Rosario told Elder Smith and his companion, Elder Volker Moulding, that she knew the Church was true but wanted to wait for her husband to be baptized with her. However, as her interest grew, he became more negative about the Church, and he opposed her baptism.

After she and the elders fasted, her husband gave his consent. Since her baptism, her twenty-year-old cousin also has joined the Church.

42

It's the Mormons

In the rough east side area of Easterhouse in Glasgow, Scotland, boys had to be members of a football team and a gang to survive. "Every time you played a team at football, you would fight them afterwards. You always had to stand and fight, because to run away brought shame to your gang."

Thomas Wark can remember his gang running away only once. About twenty gang members were playing football in the street when one of the boys yelled, "It's the Mormons!" The boys scattered, sprinting in every direction to escape. Thomas only ran because everybody else did. He thought the Mormons were a special unit of the police or some other menacing gang that he had never heard about before. But as he peered from behind a wall, all he saw were two young men with short hair and suits walking down the street. They seemed harmless. Who are these Mormons, he wondered, and why was everybody scared of them? He asked the other boys about the Mormons, and they related some strange stories.

Thomas had grown up in a strong Protestant family. He despised other religions, especially Catholicism. When he met a girl, he would first ask about her religion. If she was Catholic, he refused to have anything to do with her. During this time, he joined Freemasonry and became engrossed in that organization.

But his life changed dramatically when he met a girl different from anyone he had ever dated before. "She didn't drink or smoke, she wasn't Catholic, and she wasn't interested in anything immoral."

The young lady said she was Mormon, and her faith meant more to her than anything or anyone. He respected her principles and fell in love with her. They were married in an LDS church, but they agreed not to preach to each other. However, the death of Thomas's father a year later would provide his wife with the opportunity to preach through her example.

His family was devastated by his father's death. "I tried to get some satisfaction from two ministers . . . , [but] neither of them could help me understand death, so I became even more depressed."

Though only twenty, his wife helped pull him and his family through their bereavement. She invited two sister missionaries for dinner, and they explained the plan of salvation to him. Later they taught him the gospel. "I really fought the sisters, but they persevered and, as time went by, I began to believe this church was true. Through prayer, I knew I must give up all my worldly habits and join this great church."

On December 11, 1985, Thomas was baptized. His new faith changed more than just the way he lived; it changed his feelings toward other people. He and his wife have formed a close friendship with a Catholic couple. The bigotry of his past has been replaced by a love for the gospel and others. "I have found true happiness at last."

43

Teach Us Right Now

Elders George Darrough and Robert Russell did not expect their 4:00 P.M. appointment to last for hours. But then, they had never met a man like Hoyt G. Wilson before.

In March 1962, Hoyt, a boat salesman, was mayor of Lake Dallas, Texas, near Denton. While attending a boat show, he responded positively when a Church member asked if he'd like to know more about the Mormons.

That led to a referral and the appointment on Tuesday, March 26, 1962. As the elders taught Hoyt, along with his wife, niece, and nephew, they knew he was ready for their message. "All his life he had been waiting for this, but didn't know what it was until he heard the gospel plan," Elder Russell recalls. "He knew this was what he had been waiting for."

After hearing the first discussion, Hoyt asked whether there was any more. "We said, 'Yes, five more,' " Elder Russel recalls. "He said, 'We have plenty of time, why don't you teach us right now?' "

Midway through the discussions, Hoyt gave up smoking. Later, he asked to be baptized the next afternoon. The elders wanted to wait at least one more day. After hearing about Hoyt, Texas Mission President Ralph J. Hill wanted to wait even longer. "You can't do that; you have got to take a little more time," President Hill said. But he added that if the local branch president interviewed Hoyt and felt he was ready, he would give his permission.

"The branch president was just amazed at Hoyt's total conversion," Elder Russel says. Hoyt, his wife, niece, and nephew were baptized.

From the time of his conversion until his death, May 12, 1980, Hoyt Wilson helped bring more than a hundred people into the Church. After his baptism, he held a family reunion and asked all who attended if they wanted to know more about the Church. A niece accepted the invitation and became converted.

On another occasion, while attending a political dinner at a country club, he turned his coffee cup over and asked the man next to him if he knew why he had turned his coffee cup over.

"I guess you don't want any coffee," was the reply.

"No, it's because I joined the Mormon church," Hoyt said. "How much do you know about the Mormon church?"

44

Worth Chasing After

As Vicki Morton rode her bicycle to work one summer morning in 1981, she pondered and prayed about Mormonism. For some time, she had wanted to learn about the Church, and she didn't want to wait any longer. She asked the Lord to help her find the missionaries. As she rode up a hill, she saw two young men who looked like missionaries riding down the hill on the other side of the street. She knew her prayer had been answered. "I stopped and yelled, 'Are you missionaries?' " she remembers. "They didn't hear me. I turned around and followed them yelling, 'Stop.' They kept going. I chased after them, and I caught up with them after three blocks."

She was out of breath, and the missionaries were staring at her with shocked looks on their faces. Even people passing by in cars looked at her as if she were nuts. She didn't care about those reactions. What mattered to her was that she had found the missionaries.

Her interest in the Church had been sparked a year earlier by a friendly family of five living next door to her, her husband, Maurice, and son, Joey. The Mortons had just moved to Orlando, Florida, from Kansas in the summer of 1980. "We were impressed with how kind and friendly the family was," she says. "They always said, 'Hi' to us, and their boys liked to play with our son."

While visiting next door, Vicki learned her new neighbors were Mormons. Maurice invited the LDS family to his church, but the people responded that even though they didn't attend their meetings, they would not go to any other church. The Mortons began spending more time with their neighbors, learning a lot about what they believed. Maurice had studied religion in college, and knew that Latter-day Saints had the priesthood. Vicki's curiosity was aroused.

"We [she and her husband] were confused about all the religions that we had gone to up until now," she says. "We were looking for a church that satisfied our needs and that taught about the true gospel."

After praying for help in finding the truth, they were asked by their neighbors if they wanted to talk to the missionaries. They said yes, and looked forward to learning more. Their desire to investigate the Church grew as time passed. Still no missionaries came. "I am not a very patient person, and I knew I wanted to know more about this church," Vicki says.

She had an aunt and uncle who were Latter-day Saints, but she had been told as a child that Mormons had secrets, and she wasn't to ask any questions. But the Mormons she had known in her life seemed pretty normal. And as an adult, she was ready to get answers to her questions. When she finally cornered the missionaries, she wasn't about to let them get away without them promising to teach her about Mormonism. The missionaries were from a different area, so she gave them her name and number.

"I was twenty minutes late for work that day, but it was worth it," she says.

The next day, the Mortons were taught the first discussion, and two weeks later they were baptized. "I know that prayers are indeed answered," Vicki says. "What a joy it is to be a part of this great Church!"

45

They Went on Faith

Burgess Owens now feels that the only reason he played professional football, specifically for the then Oakland Raiders, was so he could meet Todd and Kathy Christensen.

A defensive back for the Raiders in the late 1970s and early 1980s, Burgess knew that teammates Todd Christensen, a tight end, and Marc Wilson, a quarterback, were Latter-day Saints, but he avoided talking about religion with them. "I really never broached the question before, because I had very negative impressions about Mormons," Burgess says. "I heard Mormons were racist, but I didn't want to not like Todd because of his religion. For more than two years we talked about anything but religion."

Burgess and Todd had become friends because both were family oriented. The two families began spending a lot of time together. During the 1982 pro football players' strike, Burgess's family returned to their home in New York. Anticipating the end of the strike, he was alone on the West Coast in late November. Several friends invited him over for Thanksgiving dinner, but he only accepted the one extended by the Christensens. "After we ate dinner, we went in the living room and talked as a fire burned in the fireplace," he remembers. "We didn't talk about religion that night either. We discussed families, the country, freedom and opportunities. It was a positive discussion that opened me up to the fact that they [the Christensens] were really good people. I had a good time with them."

Two weeks later his wife, Josie, returned to Oakland on a Saturday and decided to stop and visit Kathy Christensen while driving home from the airport. As she walked up to the door, she encountered two missionaries who were just leaving the Christensen home. Kathy said she had been talking to the missionaries about Josie and asked if her friend would like to attend church with her the next day. Josie accepted, went to Sunday meetings, and came away impressed, especially with Relief Society.

When her husband arrived home from an away football game that night, she shared her feelings and persuaded him to attend church with her the next Sunday. By coincidence, the Raiders were playing a Monday night game at home, a situation which freed up the only Sunday of the season that Burgess could have gone to church. What he experienced that day started an investigation that changed his life. The Church's emphasis on the father's responsibility as the patriarch of his home and on priesthood authority struck him deeply, causing him to reevaluate his misconceptions about the gospel.

"It was all new," recalls Burgess of his first LDS meeting. "Nothing negative occurred, and I thought it was nice."

He and Josie knew they had found the right church for their family. They began studying with the missionaries, whose message seemed to ring true. They were moving toward baptism with a gust of wind at their backs until they encountered an obstacle—the revelation opening the priesthood to all worthy males. Proud of his black heritage, Burgess was bothered that blacks had been refused the rights of the priesthood before the revelation.

"I stayed up until 4:00 A.M. reading the Bible and praying," he says. His faith wavered, and he felt unsure about the Church. Then the next day at a dinner the mission president leaned over to Burgess to explain how the Lord works. "He said the Lord will give you just enough to take the first step, and then the Lord wants you to take the next step on faith."

That was what Burgess and Josie needed to hear. They felt the Church was true, and they now resolved to go on faith and follow their feelings. They were baptized at 10:00 P.M. on December 31, 1982. "It's amazing how, once you take that first step, your faith just grows. Thank goodness I started that way in the Church. I feel so good about what I have right now."

Burgess has not shied away from sharing what he has found. He introduced his good friend Dwayne O'Steen, a former football player, to the gospel. Dwayne's attitude toward the Church changed from contempt to conviction as he attended meetings and saw the gospel in action. He and his wife, Chris, joined the Church, as did Burgess's brother Donald and two of Josie's brothers and a sister. Another former teammate, Bobby Jackson, and his wife, Celeste, also have been converted.

Burgess's experience of going on faith also helped him in sharing the gospel with other blacks who were struggling with the Church's stand before the priesthood revelation. He introduced the gospel to one of those, Dana Kinlaw, in 1984. Dana and his wife, Cheryl, had been searching, and they quickly gained a testimony. In 1989 Dana was called as bishop of the Uniondale Ward in New York.

As for Burgess, he has served in the stake mission presidency of the Plainview New York Stake. "Missionary work is my niche," he says with enthusiasm.

46

Mom Was Led by Her Daughter

In 1976 Gloria Wylie of Laingsburg, Michigan, was a forty-year-old single mother going through one of the worst years of her life. Now she says 1976 marked the beginning of a new life that would lead five people into the Church.

It began when her sixteen-year-old daughter, Lori, asked if she could write to the well-known singing group, the Osmonds. Lori and her nieces—Barbara, fifteen, and Linna, thirteen—had formed their own band and performed many songs sung by the Osmonds.

Gloria gave Lori permission, but said she must also ask for a statement of the Osmonds' religious beliefs. Lori mailed the letter, and the Osmonds responded with a letter and an Articles of Faith card. Gloria, who had attended many churches and studied the Bible, said the Articles of Faith seemed scripturally sound.

Lori then said she had been observing two LDS boys in her high school. "Do you suppose I could call their mom and ask for a ride to their church this Sunday?" she asked her mother.

"Little did I know that calling their mom [Rosalie Risk] would be like calling the hounds down from heaven," Gloria says jokingly. "Rosalie was, and still is, an avid missionary for the gospel of Jesus Christ. Soon, Barbara and Linna started to go to church as well."

Later, the girls asked if some elders could come to Gloria's home and teach a lesson. Gloria agreed because she liked "nice old gentlemen" and wanted to hear about her daughter's new church. "Imagine my surprise when two tall, handsome young men with regulation haircuts and business suits appeared on my doorstep at the appointed time."

Elders David Terry and Keven Crump taught the girls, and Lori, Barbara, and Linna were baptized. Later, Gloria took the three girls on a trip to Utah and spent some time with Elder Terry's family in Springville, Utah. She returned to Michigan and married James H. Wylie on March 26, 1977. A month later, the couple was also baptized.

Lori's two nieces, Barbara and Linna, came to live with the Wylies for their last years of high school. "For a few years, we had that wonderful Church family, and I was able to watch the girls grow in the gospel," Gloria says. "The girls are married now and are all active in the Church."

47

What Are We to Do?

Madame Legay, a social worker living on the western outskirts of Paris in 1960, listened as the heartbroken young family asked for her help. "What are we going to do?" they asked. "We have to have somebody take charge of the service."

Their five-month-old baby had just died without having been baptized. The ordinance hadn't been performed because the family had been waiting for the return of the child's father, a French army officer serving in Algeria. The family had tried to get their priest to conduct the funeral, but he refused, saying he couldn't do it because the child had not been baptized. According to the doctrine of the church, the infant was condemned and could not be saved.

Madame Legay, who had joined the LDS church two weeks earlier, asked the family if they would consider allowing Mormon missionaries to conduct the service. The family, who had heard the missionaries and been impressed with their message, agreed to the idea. So did the elders, despite having never conducted a funeral before. They opened the service with singing and a prayer and then preached from the scriptures about salvation for infants who die before the age of accountability. As she listened to this doctrine, the mother's countenance changed, and she began to smile. Other family members also were visibly affected by the message.

Within three months, twenty-five people were baptized as a result of the funeral. Among those taught and converted were the infant's grandparents, uncles, aunts, and cousins. By October 1961 more than a hundred people in that area had joined the Church.

During one of the baptismal services for a group of people associated with the infant's family, one of those new converts said in his testimony: "I do not know of a more wonderful work that an infant could have done in five months of life than this."

V

Book of Mormon Conversions

48

The Different Church

Crisanto D. Madriaga felt at home in many churches. His parents were members of the Philippines Independent Church, but he was baptized into the Catholic Church. At age seven he went to live with his aunt and uncle, who were childless, and there he learned about the Bible in a Protestant church.

"As I grew older, I became a free-thinker, going to all three churches," he says. Crisanto thought that being a Christian meant any religion was just the same, and attending various churches was not a problem. If one religion was criticized by someone, he jumped to its defense. As time passed, however, so did his interest in religion.

By 1969, the forty-one-year-old Crisanto spent most of his free time drinking with his friends. "I couldn't have cared less about my family; whether they could eat or not did not matter to me." But one Saturday afternoon, while he was drinking with his friends, two missionaries came to his home. Out of curiosity, he invited them in. "My friends made fun of them, but I listened to them. I tried to measure their knowledge of the Bible by asking questions."

The missionaries assured him that if he read the Book of Mormon, his questions would be answered. When they left, the missionaries promised to return the next Saturday. "During the week, I read the Book of Mormon," Crisanto recalls. "The following Saturday I waited for the two missionaries to come, but they did not arrive. And so I went out to look for this church."

Spurred on by his conscience, he became obsessed with finding "this different church." Appointments with friends were quickly forgotten as he began to seriously study and ponder religion. Why, he thought, would he feel so driven to find this church if it wasn't true? Finally, he found the Church and was soon being taught by the missionaries. He was baptized January 11, 1970.

"That was the turning point of my life. I abandoned my vices and my stupid philosophy in life that had led me to misery and debts. I became a new man in the eyes of God and accepted trials and persecution as part of my conversion in this new faith. I gained a testimony, and every time I testified during fast meeting, I cried."

After seeing the change in Crisanto, his wife also became interested in the Church and joined. On November 10, 1985, Crisanto was ordained a high priest and patriarch of the Zamboanga Philippines Stake.

49

The Best Missionaries

Conley Smith feels he was brought into the Church by some of history's greatest missionaries.

To explain, the temple worker from Mount Vernon, Washington, recalls how he was stationed by the Army in 1952 at Camp Cook, named after Philip St. George Cook (now Vandenberg Air Force Base), near Santa Maria, California. He later learned that Cook had commanded the Mormon Battalion.

One day in June 1952, Conley had kitchen duty. During a break, he rummaged through a pile of magazines at the barracks and began flipping the pages of one, stopping at an article entitled, "Peculiar People." He read the article through before returning to duty, and during the next week he read it several more times.

The story referred to a Book of Mormon. Conley went to the camp library to see if a copy was available.

"There I found a red hardbound copy of the Book of Mormon," he says. "Thumbing through, I decided to check it out more closely and found that I enjoyed reading the book."

About halfway through reading the book, he decided he wanted to see what the people "who wrote the Book of Mormon were like." On a Sunday morning he looked in the camp newspaper and found an announcement that the Latter-day Saints were meeting that afternoon. He attended, thought it interesting, and returned a week later.

"That time they had what they called a testimony meeting," he recalls. "They started on the right corner of the first row and went from person to person and from row to row. I happened to be the last person on the back row. Each person told a bit about his life in the Church. I said something about how I was enjoying reading the Book of Mormon."

Conley continued to read the Book of Mormon and attend meetings. On August 24, 1952, he was baptized. Three months later, on a troopship bound for Europe, he learned from several returned missionaries about the Church's missionary program. These former missionaries taught him a lot about the gospel. Conley enjoyed their fellowship, but he didn't regret that full-time missionaries hadn't been involved in his conversion.

"I had the best missionaries to learn from in Nephi through Moroni," Brother Smith declares. "I can testify that the Book of Mormon is true, for it was what brought me to the Church and the gospel."

50

They Sent a Sacred Book

In 1944 Normand Laub and his brother, Merril, of Newcastle, Utah, fought on the eastern Leyte beaches, during the liberation of the Philippines in World War II. Merril died there.

In the spring of 1985, Normand fulfilled a long-term dream by returning to the Philippines, visiting the beaches and the small town of Jaro, where his military unit had been stationed for many months forty-one years earlier.

Normand and his wife, Barbara, retraced the steps he had taken as a young serviceman. They found that the people of Jaro still had fond memories of the Americans who had served there during the war. The Laubs were welcomed by the townspeople and, after returning home, corresponded with many of them.

In 1986, the Laubs sent their testimonies and a cover letter to President Roy E. Boulter of the Philippines Cebu Mission, along with referral cards for five families. They also wrote to each of these families and told them they would be giving them a sacred book that would change their lives. They explained the book would be delivered by missionaries from the Church.

The referrals were passed on to Lionell and LaRue Walker, leadership trainers on that part of the island, because there were no missionaries and no Church organization in Jaro.

"We spent one day finding and visiting the referred people, placing copies of the Book of Mormon and taking photographs for our report back to the Laubs," says Elder Walker, now home in Mount Vernon, Washington. "Almost everyone we talked to remembered them, and many were waiting for their 'sacred book.' "

Three days after receiving the Book of Mormon, the Pontejos family visited the Walkers in Tacloban, thirty-five kilometers from Jaro. They said they had read part of the book, knew it was true, and wanted to join the Church.

"They were sad when we told them that it wasn't that easy, but they took additional literature and returned home to study and wait to be taught by the missionaries," Elder Walker recalls.

On April 12, 1987, the Pontejos and their three daughters were baptized. In June, missionaries were sent to Jaro to open up the area for missionary work. Because of the seeds planted by the Laubs, other people also have been baptized, and the work of conversion continues.

51

Just a Book

Until he met two sister missionaries in 1986, Fred Halupka, then of Allentown, Pennsylvania, thought it was only necessary that he succeed in life. The rest of the people could worry about themselves.

"Charity disappeared a few years before when a job I had was lost," Fred recalls. "I placed the blame of losing that job on the human race. If they weren't going to help me succeed in life, then I was not in any mood to help any of them."

But, as Fred marvels now, "just a book" would change him and give new direction and purpose to his life. Fred was introduced to the book when two sister missionaries left a copy of the Book of Mormon with him after teaching the first discussion. He had no intention of reading more than just a page or so, because that was what he had promised the sisters he would do. But the more he read in the first book of Nephi, the more he realized that other people hadn't had their lives handed to them easily either. Instead, people learned their potential and abilities through adversity.

"When I began to understand the feelings of Lehi and how it truly hurt him to see his two sons, Laman and Lemuel, not holding on to the iron rod, I could place myself into the same position and see that I was not only hurting my earthly father by living in the manner I was living, but I also was hurting my Father in Heaven."

Fred resolved to trade his selfishness for a willingness to serve others. After meeting with the missionaries for the third time in two weeks, he sought a quiet place to pray and asked if the Book of Mormon was true. He also wanted to know what he should do with his life.

"In the early evening, I sat on the steps going to the bedrooms [where he lived] and held my copy of the Book of Mormon. It was the first time I had ever tried praying in the manner the sisters taught, and I didn't know what to expect." He asked the Lord to help him decide what was true, and to help him deal with the difficulties that might arise if he received that knowledge.

"I never before felt such a comforting feeling, and every pulse in my body and every muscle was relaxed," he says. "I understood that what I was holding was of vital importance, and that I needed to do whatever was necessary to retain such a feeling."

He was baptized in 1986. In July 1987 he left on a mission to Vienna, Austria. "I feel so much closer to my Heavenly Father and those around me," Elder Halupka wrote in a letter to Allentown ward member Daniel L. Vassilaros in July 1988. "I gain so much joy in serving others. Although my earthly parents are not members yet, we also have [grown] so much closer and show our love for one another [better] than ever before. This church is my lifeline."

52

What Is That Book?

When Alberto C. Bulseco made the decision to be baptized, he knew it might mean the end of his marriage. But "I had feared God all my life," he says. "I could not reject that which I knew was true."

Alberto, who would later become president of the Sorsogon District of the Philippines Cebu East Mission, had been looking for the true church for most of his life. He first heard about the restored gospel during his summer vacation in 1980. "We stopped at the boardinghouse of my brother, who was then studying in Manila, to take a rest before proceeding further north [to where his parents lived]. I have two brothers, and we're very close. Whenever we meet, it has been our practice to discuss scriptures from the Bible and also to talk about religion. Since childhood we have been dissatisfied with the religion our parents taught."

His brother said Mormon missionaries were coming to their boardinghouse to visit one of the other residents. Alberto remembered reading about the Mormons in the past and knew they believed in an ancient, but progressive, civilization. As it happened, the person the missionaries were supposed to visit was not interested, so the two brothers entertained them instead.

The elders, one an American and the other a Filipino, started by teaching the young men to pray. Alberto offered the opening prayer. When he finished, the American missionary began explaining more about prayer, but Alberto's attention was drawn to a blue book half hidden under the Filipino elder's arm.

"I was curious," he recalls. "I interrupted the missionary and asked what the book was. They were somewhat hesitant to tell me, but I strongly felt that it had something to do with their belief." He asked for the book, promising to read it. The missionaries continued to stall, so Alberto insisted that he receive a copy and swore he would read it. The elders then gave him the book and explained a little about it before continuing their discussion.

That discussion largely went unheeded. "The next things they said were no longer important to me. I felt that this book would tell me all I needed to know from them. My enthusiasm to begin reading the Book of Mormon was so intense that I wanted to cut short my vacation."

When he and his wife and child returned home, he finally had time to read. As he opened the book, he felt some power in it that caused his fingers to tremble. "A marvelous feeling engulfed me as I read every line. I often had to repeat the words and verses just to savor the sweet and satisfying feeling that came from them. My inspiration in reading the Book of Mormon was very unusual. I almost never got tired and hungry. To eat was a burden. I woke up during the middle of the night just to read it."

No other book had caused him to weep as the Book of Mormon did. It seemed to quench his soul's thirst for spiritual truth. A month after starting it, he finished reading the book and wanted to be baptized. The missionaries in Manila had taken down his name and address and had promised to have other missionaries visit him. However, none had knocked on his door.

Finally, Alberto went searching for the missionaries. When he found them, he told them he wanted to be baptized. They were so surprised they thought Alberto was joking. But when Alberto testified of the truth of the Book of Mormon, the missionaries realized he was sincere. They began teaching him the discussions. His wife persecuted him for studying and threatened to leave him. But he said only God could stop him from being baptized.

On August 5, 1980, Alberto was baptized. "I felt a fulfillment I had never felt in my life," he said. Two years later his wife joined the Church, and they and their four children have been sealed in the temple. His parents, brothers, and one sister also have been converted. All these blessings he attributes to a faith kindled from reading the Book of Mormon.

53

They Couldn't Stop Reading

On an April evening in 1988, ten young people began reading the Book of Mormon and didn't stop until they finished the next day. Most of them later investigated the Church, and some were baptized. The catalyst sparking this remarkable Book of Mormon conversion was an LDS girl whose love for an annual Easter pageant provided an opportunity for her nonmember friends to feel the Spirit.

As Lori Christlieb attended Green River College in Seattle, she became friends with several students who were in some of the same classes and ate lunch together every day. During the winter of 1988, Lori shared with them her strong feelings for the Easter pageant, "As I Have Loved You," sponsored by the Spokane Washington North Stake. Lori was from Spokane and played the trumpet in the orchestra for the pageant. She invited the students to attend, and ten of them accepted her invitation.

On Wednesday, April 6, 1988 these ten got into a van owned by a girl named Cathy and made the five-hour drive from Seattle to Spokane. After they watched the pageant, they stayed after to compliment Lori for her efforts. Lori struggled to hide her disappointment because she had wanted everything to be perfect for her friends but knew the performance hadn't been one of their best. However, a few days later, when she returned to Seattle and opened her mail, she realized that the quality of the music had not detracted from the outpouring of the Spirit.

The letter was from Cathy but represented the feelings of all of her friends who had attended the pageant. "We truly enjoyed it," Cathy wrote. Never in Cathy's life had she witnessed such a manifestation of the Savior's love. "We got in the van and started to head home," Cathy wrote. "There was silence and pondering of what we had just witnessed—except for Jake. He kept saying, 'Those people's spirits were so overwhelming.' "

Lori had given Sylvia, another member of the group, a Book of Mormon two days before leaving for Spokane. Sylvia hadn't read anything from the book, but she had brought it along on the trip to the pageant.

"After about an hour and a half on the road, and nonstop talking about the pageant, [we had] a feeling of calm come over us all," Cathy recalled. "Nita very quietly asked if she could see Sylvia's Book of Mormon."

Nita began reading aloud.

"It was as though we were all starving for the words it contained. I pulled the van to the side of the road, and there we started at the beginning. We could not let these words leave our mind, so we continued and did not stop until we reached the last verse, Moroni 10:34: 'And now I bid unto all, farewell. I soon go to rest in the paradise of God, until my spirit and body shall again reunite, and I am brought forth triumphant through the air, to meet you before the pleasing bar of the great Jehovah, the Eternal Judge of both quick and dead. Amen.' "

They had taken turns, each reading a chapter at a time. The time that passed had seemed short, but when they finished, they discovered their reading had taken them more than sixteen hours. It was 5:16 P.M. Thursday!

Cathy then recalled the night when Lori testified to the true meaning of the pageant as a way to worship the Savior. Lori also had told them about the spiritual leadership of the director and how she motivated the musicians to be in touch with the meaning of the music they were rehearsing, so this feeling could be conveyed to the audience. In this respect, Cathy wrote, the performers had been successful. "In no way did the mistakes take away from the reverence and get in the way of us witnessing such a glorious event!

"I probably speak for everyone [in saying] we never expected to be so fully and totally moved as we were that night."

As a postscript, Cathy noted that Lori probably would be happy to hear that Scott, Ted, Kate, Sylvia, Jake, Nita, and herself had scheduled to start taking the missionary lessons as a group in Nita's home April 16, 1988. "I for one am very anxious and excited to begin," Cathy concluded.

Lori moved back to Spokane soon after the pageant. Since that eventful night, she hasn't had any contact with these friends on whom she had such a profound influence. However, she learned from another student she had known at the college that four of the ten had been baptized. She could count those as the first of many she would introduce to the gospel, for she soon became Sister Lori Christlieb serving in the Peru Lima North Mission.

54

Drawn to the Book

One night in 1965, Tim Powers surrendered to a bout of insomnia and went to the University of Montana library, where he stumbled onto a book that would change his life.

An All-American swimmer at the school, Tim relished challenges, but he couldn't deal with the ultimatum delivered by his LDS girlfriend: "She said she would marry in the temple or not marry at all."

Sure, he had enjoyed going to church with her, and the members were nice, but becoming a Mormon wasn't a step he wanted to take. These thoughts cluttered his mind and kept him awake that night in 1965.

"I was looking for a carrel to study in when I was drawn to the religious titles on the bookshelf along the aisle I was walking through. And there was a Book of Mormon. Nobody had ever given me a Book of Mormon." Tim pulled out the book, found a carrel, and began reading in First Nephi.

"I really got into it," he recalls, "I could identify with Laman and Lemuel and their unwillingness to change. It was like me. I saw all the good works in the Church, but still I had hardened my heart." His eyes filled with tears as he realized that this was the answer to his mental struggle. This spiritual awakening led to more study and prayer. On April 16, 1966, he was baptized, and the next day he was made institute president.

Later, he married Patricia Bradford, a former Miss Montana, in the Salt Lake Temple. He then entered the army, where he served in Vietnam as a courier. When he returned to civilian life, he started a swim club team in California that soon became one of the largest in the country.

His success with the club and in the high school ranks earned him a head coaching job at BYU, where he has directed a successful swimming program since 1974. Usually, about half of the team consists of returned missionaries, and Tim is just as proud of the number of team members who have joined the Church and served missions through the years as he is of the outstanding swimmers he has coached.

In 1987 he received a lot of media attention in Southeast Asia as the coach of the Singapore National Team, which included some BYU swimmers. He reflects: "In the last few years, more students from Singapore and that area of Asia are applying for school and coming [to BYU]. I definitely think I'm an ambassador for the Church and BYU."

55

He Sifted Out Facts

For forty-five years, private investigator Lawrence G. Doull II has made his living sifting facts from fiction. But no investigation changed his life like the one he began unwittingly as a youth and ended on Easter 1962 when he was baptized a member of the Church.

Lawrence first encountered the Church as a teenager in 1941 when the family traveled from California to Idaho to visit his father's birthplace in Soda Springs. The elder Doull was a "no-nonsense" exmilitary man who had joined the army at age thirteen and had also served in the marines.

During the Idaho trip, the family camped on a bluff overlooking the Snake River. The next morning they awoke to find the place swarming with Mormons. It was some ward activity, Lawrence said. The bishop and his counselors visited the Doulls' tent and invited the family to join them for a hotcake breakfast.

"When we left, Dad told me, 'If I ever join a church, it will be the Mormons, because they are not Christmas and Easter Christians,' " Lawrence recalls. "He didn't like hypocrites too much."

When his father was converted to the Church twenty years later, he arranged for missionaries to contact his son, who was then living in Glendale, California. "The missionaries were sincere and dedicated young men, and that impressed me," Lawrence says. "I didn't have any trouble with anything they presented except the Joseph Smith story." As a private investigator, he looked for two things: truth and truth. "God coming down in a beam of light to appear to a young boy from New York was a tough concept for me to accept."

Lawrence checked out almost every book the Glendale library had on the Church, both pro and con. He also read the Book of Mormon and compared it to the Bible. His study took more than a year. "I wasn't going to join until I was firmly convinced that all aspects of the Church were true. I simply had questions I couldn't resolve."

Reading the Book of Mormon marked the turning point in his conversion. He knew it was true. "Then, of course, Joseph Smith had to be a prophet. Once you read the Book of Mormon, you don't have any problems with the Joseph Smith story."

With his conversion, he began an eternal investigation, one in which there was no limit to what he could learn. "I like the approach of the Church," says Lawrence. "You are responsible for what you will be and where you will go, and the Church is going to do everything in the world to help you and give you the knowledge to become what you should."

VI

"Coincidences" of Conversion

56

Elder Wore Pink Pajamas

On April 5, 1969, during a general conference priesthood session, William "Bill" Nerenberg learned the Church was true.

Only four years before that, he had committed himself to a life of meditation, prayer, voluntary servitude, and poverty as a Benedictine Monk. But a series of coincidences or "divine interventions," as Bill calls them, led him step by step to the restored gospel.

While a student at St. Martin's College in Olympia, Washington, he became attracted to the Benedictine Order because the monks' contemplative life struck him as an ideal way to serve the Lord. However, after one year, he reluctantly left the monastery because his father had been stricken by a sudden, serious illness. His family needed him to return home to run the family business.

"Within several weeks of my return, my father recovered completely," Bill says. "He has never missed a single day of work before or since."

Leaving the monastery cost Bill his draft exemption, and he was drafted into the army. He tried to join the air force, but its quota was full, and he was placed on a waiting list. Just days before reporting to the army, Bill received word that the air force had an unexpected opening and signed him up.

Another coincidence occurred at the end of basic training when he inadvertently filled out the wrong form. Noticing his mistake, he asked for another form but was told, "Not on your life." Instead of going to his choice of assignment and training, he was shipped to March Air Force Base in the California desert.

He arrived on a hot, fall evening and was promptly escorted to his quarters. The heat inside the barracks was intense. As he walked down a long hall to his room, he saw that all of the men were clad in skivvies—except one. He was wearing pink pajamas! Bill turned and stared at the man. His escort nudged him and said: "If you think that's funny, you should see the long underwear he wears under them, too. He and some of the others belong to a strange religion, but don't worry; if you don't bother them, they won't bother you."

Bill resolved to give the fellow a wide berth, but the next day he shuddered to discover that he was assigned duty with the pink-pajama man. Curiosity soon led Bill to ask the soldier, Marshall Hatch, about his strange sleeping attire. Marshall explained that the pajamas were a gift from his mother, and he felt obligated to wear them. He wore the long underwear because he was an elder in his church.

"That did it," Bill recalls. "Marshall Hatch was all of twenty-two, and certainly not old enough to be the gray-haired senior member of the congregation that most churches identify as an elder."

For several weeks, Bill avoided any further quizzing of the returned missionary from Burley, Idaho, about his odd beliefs. But Marshall renewed Bill's curiosity by asking him if he wanted to meet some girls. Now he was interested. He attended a church activity and met several "good looking, clean, and wholesome" young women. Two weeks later Bill brought half the servicemen on his floor of the barracks to an LDS social. Many of those men would later join the Church.

At one of these socials, Bill met his future wife, Jan Marie Gombert, an investigator who already had a testimony of the gospel. She introduced him to the missionaries. "I met them and immediately liked those two young men so much that I decided to take the time to show them the error of their ways. I stayed up nights studying the Book of Mormon to help me convince them. But testimonies don't come as often when we look for error as when we look for truth. I became known in the mission district as a contact to avoid."

Bill also continued to be active in his church's youth group. "One of the most pressing problems of that time was our concern for the large number of young men who reacted to the shock of being shipped to the terror of Vietnam by turning away from all the morals they had acquired as youths and resorting to alcohol, drugs, and vice," Bill remembers. "We didn't know what to do. Our best advice—pray for them."

In April 1969, some LDS friends invited him to general conference. During the priesthood meeting, Elder Boyd K. Packer of the Council of the Twelve spoke about the challenges facing young men and women in the armed services. He outlined the Church's program for them. "As I sat there," Bill says, "I thought: 'That man is right. That [the Church's program for servicemen] is true. That's what the Lord would do.' I was baptized a month later."

57

He Hungered and Thirsted

When Robert G. Hyde and a friend enlisted in the United States Air Force in 1954, they filled out entrance papers at a recruiting office in Pendleton, Oregon.

"Hey, what are you going to put down for religion?" Robert asked.

"Mormon," said his friend, who was an inactive member.

It sounded good to Robert, even if he didn't know anything about the Church. He wrote "Mormon" in the space provided and continued filling out the rest of the application.

On the second week of basic training in San Antonio, Texas, the recruits were allowed to leave the base to attend church. "We'd do anything to get out of the barracks," Robert declares. The pair searched out the LDS church and attended meetings. "I liked church," Robert recalls. He and his friend returned together the next week, but after that the friend quit going, and Robert went alone. "Those [the people at church] were the only people nice to me during basic, and I kept going back," he said.

He began studying the Bible and information about the Church. Several weeks later, he went out on bivouac in the Texas desert. It was the middle of the summer, and once a day, at lunchtime, the soldiers received a cold drink.

"One day it was iced tea," he relates. "I had been studying that it wasn't good for you, so I gave it to someone else. Because of the heat, we weren't required to work in the hot afternoon. When I got back to my tent, I got out my little New Testament and started reading where I'd left off in Matthew, chapter 5." In verse 6, he read, "Blessed are they which do hunger and thirst after righteousness: for they shall be filled."

"I considered that [not drinking the tea] was thirsting after righteousness. It all seemed to fit together."

After being transferred to Wyoming he began studying with the stake missionaries. He was baptized on December 4, 1954, in Cheyenne, Wyoming. He was later transferred to Korea. When Robert returned home he married June Baird in Clovis, New Mexico. Later his wife was taught the gospel, and she also joined the Church.

58

He Gained a Priceless Gift

When German tourists Stefan Schmand and a friend boarded a bus in New York City, they thought they were bound for Washington, D.C., but they never arrived there. "We didn't know we were on the wrong bus until we heard passengers talking about Salt Lake City and Seattle," Stefan recalls.

By then they were halfway to the West Coast, so they kept going. Just before they arrived in Tacoma, Washington, however, their coats—containing a thousand dollars—were stolen.

Frustrated and nearly penniless, Stefan's friend called his parents in Germany and had them wire enough money for him to catch a plane home. Stefan didn't give up that easily. With only $1.50 and a heavy German accent, he went looking for a job. After no success and two breezy nights sleeping in a city park, it looked as if he would have to go home too.

"I was discouraged, but I knew things had to get better," Stefan says. "The next day a nice man observed me walking down the street with my suitcase and asked me if I wanted to go fishing with him."

The man took Stefan to meet his family, and they invited him to move in. For ten weeks he lived with the family, earning money doing odd jobs. When his host's daughter got married in Shelley, Idaho, he attended the wedding. He was impressed with the small eastern Idaho community and stayed, working at a small fireplace bellows factory and boarding with the Joey Gardner family, who were Church members. They invited him to go with them to church. Reluctantly, he went.

"The impact was immediately positive," Stefan recalls. "I never knew religion could mean so much to anyone, and I was being converted to this new way of life."

He was given a copy of the Book of Mormon in his native language and was taught the discussions by the full-time missionaries and Tom Thorpe, a German-speaking seventy in the Shelley Seventh Ward. On October 12, 1985, Stefan was baptized. Three weeks later, as he started the long trek back to Germany, forty friends from Shelley gathered at 1:30 A.M. to say good-bye.

Stefan lives in Solinger, Germany. "This country [America] robbed me of a thousand dollars, but gave me a priceless gift that can never be taken from me," he testifies.

59

His Life Turned Around

Dennis Rozell was living what he thought was a great life. He was twenty-four, single, and residing in a beautiful, wooded area near Beaumont, Texas. The beach was only a forty-five minute drive away.

One warm Saturday morning he was on his way to the sand and surf of the Gulf of Mexico when a chance encounter with two strangers changed his life. As he drove down the tree-lined highway through a sparsely populated area near his home, he saw two young men standing on the side of the road. "Both had on white shirts and wore ties," recalls Dennis, who thought the attire looked out of place on a humid morning in southern Texas. "I laughed as I neared them, wondering how people could enjoy that kind of life."

As he passed, the two young men waved, and he waved back. "I returned to thinking what a great day it was going to be," he wrote later. "But as I neared the freeway, something told me to turn around and talk to the two young men back down the road. It was a very gentle and quiet feeling. For some reason, I didn't know why, I turned around and headed back."

The missionaries were still standing where he had seen them before. Dennis couldn't think of anything to say, so he asked them who they were and what they were doing. After introducing themselves, Elders Dean G. Christensen and Dwight E. Davis explained that they were missionaries and asked if Dennis would like to learn about the Church. Dennis said yes, and an appointment was made.

"Not long after that, I was baptized into the Church," Dennis writes. Following his baptism, the missionaries told him they had been lost the day they met him.

"Even though they were lost, they had the feeling that they should wait there, so they waited," Dennis writes. "By following the gentle promptings of the Spirit and going against the world's standards, these elders caused a twenty-four-year-old to stop smoking and drinking and join the Church."

Just sixteen months after being baptized, Elder Dennis Rozell, wearing a white shirt and a tie, entered the Missionary Training Center in Provo, Utah, to prepare to teach Asians in the California Fresno Mission.

60

It Wasn't a Coincidence

A coincidence?

"Maybe," says President Corrado Misseri, first counselor in the Oshawa Ontario Stake, answering his own question. Looking back, he says one or two of the events leading to his conversion might have been considered just coincidences. "But all those things coming together at the right time and place, I believe, were guided by the hand of the Lord. It was no accident."

The "coincidences" began in 1958 when a series of crop failures forced his father, Fracesco, to give up his vineyards in Italy and move his family to Canada. Six years later, in 1964, Corrado, who was then sixteen, went to visit relatives in New York City for the summer. Some neighbor friends there invited him to go with them to the New York World's Fair.

"We went, not knowing anything about the area around the fair," he recalls. "We walked through the entrance, and the first building we saw was the LDS church pavilion. I had never heard of the Church before. Of course, the structure was fashioned after the Salt Lake Temple. I can't remember much about the pavilion, other than there were exhibits inside."

But he was impressed with the film *Man's Search for Happiness.* As he left, he filled out a referral card, checking the box indicating that he wanted more information.

"In September of the same year I received more information at my home in Toronto in the form of two missionaries—Elder Robert B. White of Calgary, Alberta, and Elder Lyman G. Ball, Jr., of California."

It was a warm fall evening. Corrado talked to the missionaries on the veranda, and they set up an appointment to teach him at the Canada Toronto Mission home.

"I think right from the beginning I could never find an argument against what they were teaching," he says. "I found their message to be reasonable. Everything just seemed to make sense."

He was baptized in October. And right away, Corrado says, he felt he belonged to his new faith. "A week after my baptism," he remembers, "I gave a talk in Sunday School and felt right at home—as if I had been doing this all my life."

61

Gifts of the Gospel

Over a hundred years ago, D.R. Gill related in a *Juvenile Instructor* story that he had grown up wishing he could have lived in the days of the Savior and enjoyed the gifts of the gospel. He hadn't realized that he would soon experience those gifts in his own life in South Wales, Great Britain.

"In the summer of 1864, some elders of the Church came and preached in front of my house," he recalled. "At the close of the meeting, one of them . . . , David Jones, gave me a tract on the first principles of the gospel, in which it was stated that the gifts of the Holy Ghost would follow the believer."

The tract caused him to think about his salvation. He wanted to know if he was going to be saved.

"I prayed to my Heavenly Father to reveal to me whether I worshipped Him aright or not," he wrote. "The first answer to my prayer was that I should be baptized by immersion for the remission of my sins."

He was attending his parents' church in Pontypridd, Glamorganshire, South Wales, and working as a miner. In November 1864 he was underground, more than a mile from the shaft, hewing coal. While meditating on the things he had heard and read about the gospel, he heard a voice telling him to go to Mountain Ash and "there it shall be told thee what thou shalt do to be saved."

"I turned around but saw nothing, and continued my work when the voice repeated the same words," he recalled. After hearing the voice for the third time, he dropped his pick and went home.

The next morning he caught the first train to Mountain Ash, a town about eight miles away.

"In the first house I entered in the settlement there were four Latter-day Saints conversing together," he said. "They were all strangers to me but one. . . . A conversation arose between us about religion, and these persons explained to me in detail the plan of salvation. My humble prayer was answered. If we will only bow ourselves before the Lord and pray from our hearts, we can all have a testimony for ourselves to know that this is the work of God."

VII

The Spirit Converts

62

He Wished It Could Be True

When Don Kruckenberg first began investigating the Church, he told his stepfather a little about the things he had learned. He expected his stepfather to respond with anger, disgust, or disappointment. "My stepfather was born in south Russia and was a strong Lutheran," Don says.

Instead of getting angry, the stepfather listened to what Don had to say, and then told him of the great faith of the Mormon pioneers. This reaction surprised Don and gave him courage to continue a course that would lead to breaking with family tradition and joining another faith.

Don's road to the restored gospel began in 1961, when he left North Dakota and went to work in Glasgow, Montana. There he became active in a large church with about fifteen hundred members and was elected to its ruling council. As the newest and youngest member of the parish leadership, he felt obligated to know the scriptures. He, his pastor, and others studied the Old Testament with great zeal.

"Through that study I became impressed with the idea of prophets," he says. "I thought, 'Wouldn't it be nice if we had prophets today.' "

In 1963 he drove by an LDS meetinghouse and saw the name —The Church of Jesus Christ of Latter-day Saints.

"I thought, 'Boy, those people have a lot of nerve!' And then I wondered if maybe they really did have something."

Don entered the navy in 1964. When he had a layover in Salt Lake City, Utah, on the way to his assignment at Lemoore Naval Air Station near Fresno, California, he visited Temple Square, and he came away with more questions than answers. Later he met a sailor who had married a former Miss Utah. He didn't know whether the sailor was a Church member or not, but the man urged him to read the Book of Mormon. Don said he would consider reading it only after finishing the Bible.

A year later he was assigned to a destroyer, where he met Dave Edens and Dale Turman, both Latter-day Saints. The pair invited Don to a cottage meeting, where two young men "with the same first names" taught a group of six to ten sailors.

"I was impressed with what they said," Don relates. "I thought it sounded pretty good, but I also felt I had to be careful about this. However, it was exciting, and I wished it could be true."

Don had struggled in grade school and had never been a good reader. Up until that time he had read only one book from cover to cover. Dale gave him a Book of Mormon, and he read it and several pamphlets. When he had read chapter 17 of 3 Nephi, he turned to Dale, who was reading on the bunk next to him. "With tears in my eyes, I said, 'I know the Book of Mormon is true.' "

Don began attending church, and soon was taking the missionary discussions. He recruited another sailor, Danny Jones, to study with him. While Don was away attending his stepfather's funeral, Danny was baptized. Another sailor, George Columbo, who had seen the Mormon Pavilion at the New York World's Fair, asked Don to tell him about the Church. George was baptized three weeks later. Don was baptized June 3, 1967.

With emotion in his voice, Don, who lives in Fargo, North Dakota, describes his conversion as a dream that became reality. "If I had my wish, I'd like to share my testimony with the world that the gospel has been restored, and we do have a prophet on the earth."

63

A Well-Placed Pen

One day back in the 1930s, Elder Louis G. Tremelling and his companion couldn't find a seat aboard a noisy bus in Buenos Aires, Argentina. As the missionaries stood near the door, Elder Tremelling watched a tall young man with an athletic build dispense bus tickets. He had a money-bag, a ticket dispenser, and a notebook attached to a clipboard for keeping a record of each transaction.

"All at once I could see he was in trouble," Elder Tremelling recalls. As he moved up for a closer look, the elder heard the young man say he had lost his pencil and would lose his job unless he kept an accurate record of his transactions.

"I don't know what impelled me to reach into my pocket and give him my new pen—which I had just purchased that day," Elder Tremelling says. He handed the pen to the ticket dispenser, explaining, "You need it more than I do."

"Who are you?" the young man asked. The Americans told him that they were missionaries from The Church of Jesus Christ of Latter-day Saints.

"Where do you live?"

They said they lived in Haedo, a small town outside of Buenos Aires.

"I live there too," was the response.

Two days later, the young man found the missionaries' residence and returned the pen. His name was Samuel Boren. Before he could leave, the missionaries asked him if he would allow them to visit his home and teach him and his family the restored gospel.

"You surely can," he said without hesitation.

Three weeks later, on September 12, 1936, he and his parents and family were baptized. Shortly after that, Samuel served a mission in Argentina. He later married Clara Angela Lorenzi.

In the years that followed, Samuel became a successful building manager for the Church in South America and for business interests in North America.

He also has helped build the kingdom. Since joining the Church, Samuel has served as a mission president in Mexico and twice in Italy. He also has been a Regional Representative.

In 1985 he was called as the first president of the Lima Peru Temple. Among those called as officiators at the temple were Louis and Isabel Tremelling from Idaho Falls, Idaho.

64

Never Lose Your Faith

Sandra L. Nichols was talking to a friend about books when two LDS missionaries who lived nearby overheard the conversation. "You enjoy reading?" one asked.

"Yes," she replied.

"I have just the book for you," said the missionary as he rushed to his car. He pulled out a copy of the Book of Mormon, brought it back, and handed it to her.

"That wasn't fair," Sandra says. "He simply smiled at me, then opened the book to 3 Nephi and asked me to read."

"You won't convert me, Elder," she said. "He smiled at me and said, 'I won't.' Later, I learned that he meant that the Spirit would [convert me]."

On May 28, 1981, she was baptized. But her husband, Raymond, was far behind. He would find a reason to be out of the room when the elders came. He didn't object to their coming, but he had no interest in hearing their message.

Six months after baptism she recieved her patriarchal blessing, in which she was promised that if she remained faithful she would enter the temple and be sealed to her family.

"I remember looking at the patriarch and saying 'Oh, Patriarch, I wish I could believe that I will someday have the opportunity to go to the temple with my family. But you just don't know my husband.' "

The patriarch smiled and said, "Where's your faith, Sister? Those weren't my words, but the Lord's. I may not know your husband, but be assured the Lord does."

The following summer, the Nicholses vacationed in Utah. While they were visiting Temple Square in Salt Lake City, Raymond told his wife he noticed a special feeling about the place. A year later, while waiting for a home teaching visit, Sandra was swept by a feeling of love and warmth for her husband. She asked him if he would listen to the missionaries to see what they were teaching their children.

"I fully expected him to reject the thought," she said. But he agreed, promising nothing but to listen. Later that night, her home teacher, Don Butts, mentioned that he too had had the same impression. She said her husband had accepted her request only minutes earlier. Don wiped a tear from his eye. "Do you feel the Spirit that's working here tonight?" he asked. Three months later Don baptized Raymond.

Before the Nicholses' August 1984 temple sealing, Sandra Nichols saw the patriarch again, introduced him to her husband, and recounted his conversion. The patriarch took both their hands and said, "Never lose your faith, Sister. Never lose your faith."

65

He Only Wanted to Listen

In the early 1970s, Glenn Kollars and his daughter took a tour of Temple Square while passing through Salt Lake City, Utah. "I remember commenting to my daughter at the time, 'I feel something sacred here,' " Glenn recalls.

Nevertheless, about six years later when two LDS missionaries knocked on his door he didn't even think about his visit to Temple Square. "One of my motives for letting them in was to show them where they were being led astray," he remembers. "But the biggest reason was a small voice whispering in my mind, telling me to at least listen to them; I didn't have to join their church."

Glenn was satisfied with his religion and felt his was the only true church, but he kept an open mind as the missionaries recounted the events leading to the restoration of Christ's church. They explained that if he wanted to know whether what they were saying was true, he needed to study and learn more about this restoration. Then, they assured him, the Lord would reveal it through the Holy Spirit. Before the missionaries left, they read from John 15:26: "But when the Comforter is come, whom I will send unto you from the Father, even the Spirit of truth, which proceedeth from the Father, he shall testify of me."

Glenn did as the missionaries asked, but was confused about how he would receive his answer. "Every night, as I would study the Book of Mormon, my heart would burn with joy and dance with happiness," he relates. "I thought, 'What a wonderful feeling,' but I couldn't understand why I was getting these unexplainable sensations."

The missionaries tried to persuade him to attend church meetings, but he refused. But night after night, the burning continued.

Glenn became convinced that the Holy Ghost was testifying that what he was reading was true. During his seven-month investigation of the Church, he prayed and studied every night. In his home of Lincoln, Nebraska, he consulted with priests, ministers, rabbis, and even theologians at the University of Nebraska. "Then the missionaries asked me again to go with them to church. By now I was getting really convinced that what they were telling me was true, so I told them that I would go with them just to see what they did, and how the service was conducted."

At the meeting, when one of the members spoke, a feeling entered Glenn's heart and filled his body with an indescribable joy. "At first I thought I was having a heart attack or something drastic was happening to my body," Glenn explains. "But then after a few moments I realized this was the answer I had been praying for. . . . From that moment my life changed. I have never been the same person from that time until this very day. The Lord had spoken through his Holy Spirit to a 'nobody' like me. How I loved the Lord for giving me this great experience!"

Two days later the elders challenged him to be baptized, and he accepted. He was baptized March 18, 1978. Two months later his daughter began studying with the missionaries and was baptized.

66

Led by the Promptings

LDS missionaries hadn't been in Heybridge or Maldon, in Essex, England, for many years, so the appearance of two well-groomed American elders from California sparked a lot of talk in the area.

The townspeople greeted the missionaries politely but turned them away time after time because they didn't need an "American" religion, recalls Sharon Everitt. "My parents took the missionaries under their wing—friendshipping them, feeling sorry that they were not being received graciously."

The elders began teaching the family the discussions. Sharon was more sympathetic than interested, having had a negative experience with organized religion at age twelve.

She felt that the concept of God had been created in men's minds in order to manipulate other people. But the eighteen-year-old listened to the young Californians. "I was curious but certainly was not searching for any kind of crutch to help me through my life," she wrote later. "I felt that maybe I could help them to understand what life was all about."

Following a few discussions, however, she was the one unsure of what life was all about. Questions were cascading into her mind.

At that time she was struggling to concentrate on her secondary school finals. "After my examinations, I committed myself to go to church. I don't know why. I still didn't believe in God. The elders had halfway given up trying to formally teach my family because my parents weren't too interested, and I found too many faults with Church teachings. I would not pray. I would not read. Yet I couldn't help but feel the promptings of something."

She attended church despite fears created by the erroneous rumors floating around her town. The LDS meetings inspired her to study the gospel more earnestly and to attend institute classes in Romford, Essex.

Through prayer, study, and church attendance she came to realize that God and Jesus Christ lived and that they loved her. In 1981 she was baptized. Less than a week later, she was accepted into the London College of Printing. Two years later she graduated with honors and began working as an assistant editor of a magazine.

At twenty-three she accepted a call to the California San Bernardino Mission, where then President Melvin Gourdin said she had a great influence on the people.

A Wise Vacation

During the summer of 1986, Fred and Carol Minnis of Dubuque, Iowa, wanted one last chance to take a long vacation with their youngest son, Brad.

Brad was to attend college soon, and his parents felt they wouldn't have another opportunity to take a lengthy trip with him. Brad asked his best friend, Vince Buss, to come along. But Vince, then a priest in the Dubuque Ward, was to go on a mini-mission that summer.

Vince and Brad had discussed religion for some time, and Vince felt he might do missionary work while on vacation with the Minnis family. His bishop, Dennis C. Manhart, wasn't so sure. "I tried as hard as I could to persuade him to go on a mini-mission instead of going on a trip with his friends," Bishop Manhart recalls. "But he convinced me, and I now believe Vince was inspired to go on the vacation. He really spent his time wisely."

Brad was searching for something, and traveling four weeks through California, Oregon, and Washington with Vince turned a curiosity about the Church into a deep desire to know whether it was true.

"During the first week in San Diego, California, Vince got me to pray," Brad remembers. "I've been praying ever since and haven't missed a day. Then, during the second week, he got me started reading the Book of Mormon. At the end of the third week, while talking in a tent, I said I wanted a temple marriage. In my mind, I was already committed to joining the Church. After that it was just a matter of learning more about it."

When they arrived home, the young men leaned on Carol Minnis's love of history to influence her to join Brad and the

Busses in attending the "City of Joseph" pageant in Nauvoo, Illinois. "That was the beginning for me," Carol says. "I saw all these people and felt something. I thought, 'This is a real community.' I was just in awe."

When she returned home, she began attending Church meetings and started taking the discussions. "Then I started wishing my husband would come with me."

Fred, an administrator at a local power company, watched his son and wife become more and more involved in the Church and knew in his heart it was right. But he wasn't sure he wanted to make the commitment. Twenty years earlier, while they were in college, Fred and Carol had been taught by two missionaries. "I received everything as being true, but I can't explain why I didn't get baptized," he says.

The turning point for him occurred when some people called to say they were coming over to visit the Minnis family on Sunday. "I told them I wouldn't be here Sunday because I was going to church," Carol recalls. "I said, 'Maybe Fred will be here.' When I asked him, he looked at me, paused, and said, 'No, I'm going to church.' "

"If the Dubuque Ward has a strength," said Bishop Manhart, "it's the friendliness of the members." The Minnis family felt welcome the minute they walked into the meetinghouse. "They're definitely a spiritual people," Fred says.

As for Vince and Brad, Vince served a mission in Norway, and Brad shared his testimony as a missionary in Argentina.

VIII

Long-Time Conversions

68

He Picked "Mormons"

When Cadet Joe Tiemann selected a topic for a comparative religion class report, he looked down the long list of religious denominations and stopped at The Church of Jesus Christ of Latter-day Saints. "I don't know why I picked Mormons," Joe says. "I can't really give you a good reason. I can say I knew some LDS cadets [at the Air Force Academy]. One of them I knew pretty well, and I thought a lot of him. After I took on this particular project, I asked him several questions about Mormons."

It was 1970. Joe was a junior at the U.S. Air Force Academy in Colorado Springs, Colorado. In three years at the academy, his feelings about religion had changed dramatically. As a youth in Karnes City, Texas, he had attended the Southern Baptist Church with his family. But since coming to the academy, he had joined a nondenominational evangelical organization known as the Navigators. At that time, he felt membership in a particular denomination was not as important as one's relationship with God. So why was he researching the Mormons? Curiosity. Joe found the study of different religions fascinating.

Books on Mormons were plentiful. Most were objective, but some were critical and negative. Although he tried to maintain objectivity when he presented his report, Joe found himself agreeing more with the perception propagated by the anti-Mormon books.

In 1971 he graduated, then spent two months touring the western United States with a friend before reporting to McClellan Air Force Base in Sacramento, California. They stopped off in Salt Lake City and toured Temple Square. Their tour guide happened to be president of a local bank. "He was a very intelligent and articulate man who said a lot of things that, at first, I did not understand," Joe says. "But when he gave scriptural references for those doctrines, I would check them out, and he would be accurate. I couldn't understand why I had never seen [those scriptures] before."

After the tour, Joe and his friend wandered around the visitors' center and met a tour guide who was a retired army colonel. The young second lieutenants were awed by this former "full colonel." He left an indelible impression on the young men. For the next few days, Joe and his friend read through each of the pamphlets and discussed the Church's doctrines and beliefs. "After two or three days, we decided the Mormons were still incorrect," Joe says. "I kind of put the issue to rest, but something continued to gnaw at me, especially when I came across one of those Bible verses quoted by our tour guide."

At McClellan, he began attending a large fundamentalist church, and soon became one of the leaders of its 125-member youth group—even though he hadn't joined that denomination. He had fun but received little spiritual satisfaction. Once during a religious retreat, Joe met a prominent anti-Mormon minister, who was the guest speaker. "He came for a week and talked about every cult. I really was disturbed by and had objections to his attitude toward Mormons. It wasn't that I disagreed with his scriptural dissertation, but I really disagreed with his attitude because I thought it was not Christian."

At Joe's next duty assignment in Alaska, his insatiable desire to understand what other people believed led him to study the Eastern Orthodox faith. Meanwhile he also met Dale Goetz, a second lieutenant and returned missionary. Goetz's positive influence succeeded in keeping Joe interested in Mormonism.

From Alaska, Joe was transferred to Germany, where he continued to immerse himself in the Eastern Orthodox religion. He also studied Catholicism. But then he met two Mormon elders. "I was driving home from work in this blowing, driving snowstorm, and I saw two missionaries walking at what seemed to be a forty-five-degree angle against the wind," Joe relates. "I thought, 'I know who these guys are.' "

He picked the elders up and gave them a ride to his apartment. "I know why you're here, and I understand what you believe," he told the missionaries. "If you're ever over in my neighborhood, drop by." A couple of days later, the missionaries visited him, and others continued to drop by for more than a year. They gave him copies of the Book of Mormon, *Jesus the Christ, The Articles of Faith, A Marvelous Work and a Wonder,* and *The Restored Church.* From reading those books and talking with the missionaries, he developed a list of objections. However, when he returned to reading the Bible, he began seeing things in a different light and understanding scriptures in a way he had never done before. "I would see things in passages of scripture that I had memorized, and it was like seeing it from a totally new perspective."

A new set of missionaries would often ask him if he had prayed about the Church. "I felt like smacking them," he says. Of course, he had prayed. For him, accepting the Church wasn't a matter of getting a yes or no answer to prayer. He could believe some of the doctrines, but he refused to surrender on the big issue—the nature of God. To abandon his belief in the Trinity struck him as the ultimate heresy.

He left Germany with a desire to continue investigating the Church. Some of his Protestant friends found this interest in Mormons disturbing. He moved to San Antonio, Texas, and Randolph Air Force Base. Two months after buying a house, he was tracted out by two missionaries. "What took you so long?" he said. The missionaries began visiting regularly, often bringing stake missionaries, the local elders quorum president, and the bishop. Joe kept up his personal study by going to the local library and picking up eight to ten books on Mormonism, including *Gospel Ideals* by David O. McKay.

"Each day I read one chapter [of *Gospel Ideals*] at lunchtime, and, each time, I would come away thinking, 'What he is saying is true. If people live like this, they will be following Christ.' "

He continued studying for four or five months. One of those working with him was Sergeant Jim Edwards, a seventy whom Joe liked. Finally, Jim challenged Joe to be baptized. "You understand as much about the Church as I do," Jim said.

"I was waiting for him to say pray about it, so I could smack him, but he didn't. He said, 'Have you fasted about it?' and I said I hadn't."

Jim said he would fast until Joe found out whether the Church was true or not. It only took one day. Joe read through the New Testament and gained many new insights. He then prayed to gain a conviction that the Church was true. First, he accepted the general idea of prophets being called of God to direct His kingdom here on earth. From Joe's reading of the Book of Mormon, he knew Joseph Smith was a prophet. His existing testimony of David O. McKay's calling helped him realize that the Church continues to be led by a prophet. "Those three principles established a foundation," Joe recalls. "I called up Jim Edwards to tell him that I had made a decision to be baptized on Sunday."

On October 12, 1980, ten years after he began his study of Mormonism, Joe was baptized.

69

A Spaniard Finds the Truth

When John Nicholson first met Mileton Gonzales Trejo in July 1874 in Salt Lake City, he was surprised to find the Spaniard didn't look anything like he expected. John anticipated a man with a swarthy complexion, dark hair, piercing black eyes, and a haughty manner. Instead, the Spaniard to whom he was introduced stood a bit below what John considered average height. He was slender and had clear, blue eyes, light hair, and a beard. "His whole makeup was attractive," John later wrote.

The Spaniard struggled to speak English, but his tone of voice was soft and appealing and his story enthralling. Mileton recounted how his father had been a colonel in the Spanish army in the mid 1800s. But the father wanted something better for his son; he urged him to serve God and not the military.

When Mileton was fourteen, his father took him to a convent so he could begin his training for the ministry. But the boy protested and cried, causing his father to relent and take him back home. Five years later, Mileton did follow his father, but this time it was into the Spanish army. Mileton was commissioned as a lieutenant.

During the early part of his military career he met an artillery lieutenant named Barrueco who spoke of a people known as Mormons in the western part of America. Barrueco said the organization of this Mormon church was the same as that in the days of Moses—directed by a prophet to whom God spoke. In time, the officer believed, this church would govern the earth.

Barrueco's words captivated Mileton. He resolved that such a people would be his people and that he would go to them or "die on the road." He requested a transfer to the Philippines, hoping it would be a stepping-stone to the United States. In 1872 he received that transfer, and while passing through France he discovered an LDS pamphlet left by missionaries. What he read shed much more light on this mysterious American religion and increased his desire to go to the Rocky Mountains.

Once in the Philippines, however, Mileton's thoughts of the Mormons and going to the United States were superseded by the pursuit of wealth. Mileton became a successful colonizer and began to have second thoughts about his desires to join the Mormons. He even felt like a traitor to his family and country. Praying for relief from his confusion, he received a soothing sensation and knew the Latter-day Saints were the people of God.

He had to go now. The governor rejected his first application for an eight-month leave, but when that governor was replaced, Mileton reapplied and received approval. In July 1874 he arrived in Salt Lake City where he met a Spanish-speaking French convert named Blanchard. Through Blanchard he became acquainted with John Nicholson, who urged Blanchard to introduce Mileton to President Brigham Young. Mileton met the prophet and was soon baptized. Later he was called on a mission to Mexico and helped establish the LDS colonies there.

But Mileton's greatest contribution to the Lord's work was his knowledge of Spanish. He translated many tracts into Spanish and helped in the translation of the Book of Mormon.

Find Those Elders

An item in the Portland, Oregon, *Oregonian* in August 1898 jarred Jens Westergaard. "Two Mormon elders who have been proselyting in the Portland area have decided to return to Salt Lake City and report that the Portland area was not a fertile field for establishment of the Church," the newspaper reporter had written.

Jens and his wife, Petrine, had been converted to Mormonism in Denmark nearly twenty years earlier, before they were married, but had never been baptized. Jens had immigrated to Utah, where he was later joined by Petrine. They were married in Ogden, Utah, on October 9, 1887, and they eventually settled in Portland.

When Jens read about the missionaries' dilemma, he and Petrine were visiting friends. They promptly cut short their visit and rushed home. Jens jumped on his bicycle and headed out in search of the missionaries. "Now, you pump, and you don't stop pumping until you find those elders," Petrine admonished as he left the house.

Jens searched all night before finding the missionaries' hotel. There he left his last twenty-five cents and a note that asked the elders to get in touch with him. Elders Joseph G. Nelson and W. J. Barnes responded. "I became a [benefactor] to them as Frederick the Wise of Saxony [did] to Martin Luther," Jens recorded. "They were without purse or scrip, and stayed in my house."

On August 30, 1898, Jens was baptized in the Willamette River. Petrine was baptized a week later.

The first Church meetings in Portland were held at the Westergaard home on Gladstone Avenue. Jens accepted a call as Portland's first branch president.

A meeting hall was rented in the Alisky Building in downtown Portland for eighteen dollars a month, which was often paid out of President Westergaard's pocket. He later served for three years as a missionary in his native Denmark. When he returned, he was again called as branch president.

71

Unforgettable Boarders

Eight-year-old Ruby Pippy and her mother were in the kitchen when they heard an explosion coming from the second floor of their home in St. John's, Newfoundland. "We went tearing up the stairs to find the missionaries covered with rice and doubled up on the floor in a fit of laughter," Ruby recalls. "Apparently they were cooking in a pressure cooker on a hot plate and had no idea how much rice to use or how high the temperature should be."

The year was 1949, and Ruby's mother had rented out the second story of their large home to the missionaries. Her mother considered the elders "her boys," treating them like sons.

"My father was completely against the missionaries," says Ruby, "and avoided them as much as possible. For this reason we never had any lessons, but we were taught [the gospel] mostly by example from all the wonderful missionaries who came to live in our home."

Ruby remembers one Sunday when the missionaries wanted to hold Sunday School but didn't have any place for the meeting or any people to attend. "They sat us five children on the top stairs, and we were the congregation," she remembers. "They gave us a beautiful talk. To this day that stands out in my mind as one of the reasons I decided to find out more about the Mormon church when I became older."

After the missionaries had boarded in the home for two years, they left. Ruby then had no contact with the Church for eleven years. At nineteen she was training at a general hospital to become a nurse when one of her instructors asked class members to do a study on different religions. She volunteered to learn more about the Mormons.

At home she found some books and pamphlets left by the missionaries more than a decade earlier. After reading the material, she talked her sister into attending an LDS meeting the next Sunday. The dusty, old town hall where they met wasn't impressive, but the service—the passing of the sacrament, the same kind of young, devoted missionaries—kindled in Ruby a thirst to learn more. Her sister was soon baptized. Because her parents asked Ruby to wait until she was twenty-one, she joined the Church two years later in 1962.

In September 1963 Ruby married Francis Pottle. He also was a convert, and they have since helped bring all his brothers and sisters, his mother, and many other relatives into the Church.

72

He Was Never Bothered Again

When he entered army basic training, Thomas J. Tedeschi was assigned to a barracks room with four men from Salt Lake City, Utah. "As we were sitting in the barracks talking to each other," Thomas recalls, "I noticed their religious preference statement was very long, so I asked, 'What is that?' They started talking to me a little about the Church, its history, and about Joseph Smith."

During the sixteen weeks of basic training, Thomas read a little in the Book of Mormon and discussed the Church with the LDS soldiers. But he had no desire to learn more. "They talked so much about how great Salt Lake and Brigham Young University were that I became totally turned off," he recalls. "When I was stationed in Germany, I used to look at the *Stars and Stripes* each day to see if BYU had lost."

While in Germany, he saw two missionaries riding through the army post and stopped them to find out who they were. When he learned they were Mormons, he said he had heard about the Church but wasn't interested. Upon discharge from the army, he returned to California and enrolled in college. He began dating a young woman, only to discover, when she refused to go with him to a Sunday event, that she was a Latter-day Saint. For a while, he stopped dating her. But later they started going out again. One night, she said, "May I ask you just one thing? Will you listen to the missionaries?" Thomas agreed on two conditions. "One was that we meet at a neutral place and not where I lived. And the second condition was that they promise never to bother me again. I was worried that the missionaries would start knocking at my door, and I would be seeing them all the time."

The appointment was set for them to meet in the college library. Thomas arrived early, and twice almost left before the missionaries came. But he stayed and listened. The things the missionaries taught him that day struck a deep chord within him. Their words helped to rectify feelings that had haunted him since his youth. "My grandfather was a minister in the Christian Assembly of God churches. He founded the North America Italian/Christian Church. He opened a mission for that church in Denver, Colorado, in the late 1950s. I was always close to my grandparents, and I was expected by the family to become a minister in their church. However, I had too many questions that could not be adequately answered. When I talked with the missionaries, I asked all the questions I had while growing up. Their answers sounded true and seemed to be what I thought to be true."

Three weeks later he finished the Book of Mormon, put Moroni's promise to the test, and received a witness of the Spirit. He was baptized June 12, 1975. On November 10, 1985, he was sustained as first counselor in the Akron Ohio Stake presidency. At that time, he was chief of audiology at a children's hospital in Akron. "The gospel changed my life completely," he says. "It gave me a lot of worthwhile goals and made me set my priorities. To be perfectly frank, without the gospel I don't think I would have ended up in my profession."

73

There's Something about Them

Years ago, an LDS missionary asked Keith Rouna whether he wanted to live with his wife for eternity.

"The question made me angry," says Keith, who thought the elder was questioning his love for his wife, Yvonne. He asked the missionaries to leave.

More than two decades later, two elders from the Massachusetts Boston Mission knocked on the Rounas' door in Brunswick, Maine. The retired navy commander was courteous, recalling the Mormon families he had known while stationed in Hawaii and Panama. But he told the missionaries, "I'm really not interested myself, because I'm an assistant minister in a local church."

"How about your wife?" asked one elder.

"She wouldn't be interested, either," Keith responded. At the time he didn't know his wife had filled out a referral card at the Idaho Falls Temple while in Rexburg, Idaho, attending a business training session. When she returned to Brunswick, she told him about attending an LDS meeting. "These Mormons—there's something about them," she exclaimed.

"What are you really looking for?" Keith asked his wife.

She replied, "I don't know, but when I find it, I'll know it."

When he told her about the missionaries' visit, she telephoned the elders and set up an appointment at her place of business. Six months later she joined the Church. Later, in a Valentine card, she asked her husband if he would meet the missionaries.

"I agreed because I felt I needed to understand her religion," he says. At first "I tried to teach the missionaries, but they just sat there and didn't argue. They just returned love. It's so difficult to argue with someone who is giving you love in return."

As the missionaries taught him, many lifelong beliefs "started crumbling around me. I felt I had known the scriptures, but I found I only knew a little, even in my position [as a lay minister]."

After receiving a "peaceful release with deepest regrets" from his former church, Keith was baptized on June 14, 1984. On July 13, 1985, he and his wife were sealed in the Salt Lake Temple.

In retrospect he says, "I have never felt as close to our Savior Jesus Christ as I do now."

74

Thrown in the Rubbish

Nineteen-year-old Carline Mason was traveling by herself through New Zealand in 1975 when a big, white building on top of a hill caught her attention.

Out of curiosity, she walked up to the New Zealand Temple. "I had never heard of the Church, except for occasionally passing an LDS chapel near my home in Adelaide, Australia," Carline says. "Of course, when I arrived at the door of the building, they wouldn't let me inside."

She was directed to the visitors' center, where an American lady showed her around and told her about Joseph Smith. "I had never thought about modern revelation," she recounts, "except on rare occasions when I thought how nice it would be to be visited by a divine being; but this was not one of those occasions."

Carline wasn't impressed with the tour. "I didn't believe a word of it. I thought, 'Just another upstart American religon.' "

She was trying to think of a polite way to excuse herself, when she saw a large picture on the wall with a family looking up to the sky and the Salt Lake Temple in the background.

"Subconsciously, it must have impressed me with its display of light, peace, family unity, and a certain sense of a greater hope and inspiration than I understood at the time."

Despite her skepticism, Carline accepted a copy of the Book of Mormon from the American lady, whose pleasant disposition was much different from Carline's stereotype of Americans. However, after she left she considered the added weight of the book in her forty-pound backpack and "threw it in the rubbish."

Five years later, two missionaries knocked on Carline's door. They met a more religious young woman than the one who had visited New Zealand, for she recently had gained a strong testimony of Jesus Christ. Again out of curiosity, she let them in. Six weeks later she joined the Church.

In October 1984, Carline returned to the New Zealand Temple Visitors' Center to find out the name of the American guide who had introduced her to the Church. Carline had just completed training for service as a missionary in the Australia Brisbane Mission, and she wanted to let the American lady know her missionary efforts had paid off.